LAUGHTER AT LAW

LAUGHTER
AT LAW

by
STANLEY JACKSON

with illustrations by
GUS

ARTHUR BARKER LIMITED
20 NEW BOND STREET LONDON WI

PRINTED IN GREAT BRITAIN
IN 12 ON 13 BEMBO
BY EBENEZER BAYLIS AND SON, LIMITED
THE TRINITY PRESS, WORCESTER, AND LONDON
27/5201

To
Julie Margaret Browne

CONTENTS

1*

Foreword
by Lord Birkett

IT is recorded of Chief Justice Erle that he once observed in what must have been an intolerably dull case (for the phenomenon does occur) that 'the Court is very much obliged to any learned gentleman who beguiles the tedium of a legal argument with a little honest hilarity'. Mr. Stanley Jackson, I feel sure, would have won his warm approval with the present anthology of amusing stories, gathered from many sources, and exhibiting the versatility of the Bench and Bar in many generations.

In his Introduction, Mr. Jackson suggests that so far as robust humour is concerned, the former times were better than these. That may well be so; but I think there will always be a place for the delicious wit of a Lord Bowen, and the spontaneous humour of the Frank Lockwoods and the Theo. Mathews of the profession. Humour of the highest kind can find its way into a profound legal judgment as Lord Macnaghten and Mr. Justice Maule have so delightfully shown. Two of my own colleagues in the Court of Appeal, Cyril Asquith and Raymond Evershed, will always remain in my thankful remembrance for the manner in which they enlivened what otherwise might have been somewhat sombre days. When Lord Evershed was discussing the nature of a particular contract, he said in the course of the argument and without premeditation—'This contract is so one-sided that I am astonished to find it written on both sides of the paper.' As a criticism it was perfect and the form made it memorable. When Mr. Justice Cassels was at the Bar and was making an application for a case to stand out of the List for a prolonged period, and Mr. Justice McNaughton had said in mock horror, 'But Mr. Cassels, all the judges of the King's Bench Division might be dead by then,' Mr. Cassels said very sweetly, 'Oh! my Lord, that would be too much to hope for'—and found his application granted.

Humour should be used sparingly in the Courts, and avoided altogether in the criminal courts, if possible; but I know of no evening so full of delight as when a company of lawyers talk the best kind of legal shop after dinner in the Temple or at the Bar Mess. When old John Nyren wanted to express the pleasure he had had in the company of the Hambledon men at the old Bat and Ball Inn, he fell back, oddly enough, on Isaac Watts and said:

> 'I have been there and still would go;
> 'Twas like a little Heaven below,'

and I share the feeling when I recall the wit and humour of those nights when some of the stories in this book came into being. Mr. Jackson has tried to trace the original authors but it is a hopeless quest.

I well remember the enjoyment with which I first heard that F. E. Smith used to drink two pints of beer at lunch time 'to bring himself down to the level of the Bench' as he said, only to discover in my later reading that a Serjeant Wilkins had said the same thing in his day, and that two hundred and fifty years before that, Sir John Millicent, a Cambridgeshire Judge, had used the same words when asked how he got on with his judicial brethren. Accuracy, too, is not to be expected when sayings are continually repeated. Only a few weeks ago I was asked by a correspondent where I had said that 'The courts are open to all—like the Ritz Hotel' and I was compelled to answer that it had been attributed to Mr. Justice Mathew but that thirty years ago it was attributed to Lord Bowen and also to Lord Justice Chitty.

When the president of the Court of Appeal said despairingly to Counsel—'But Mr. Jones, you must give this Court credit for knowing something,' and Counsel replied 'That's exactly the mistake I made in the court below', sometimes it is made to happen in England but sometimes it takes place in the Supreme Court at Washington; and when Mr. Justice Darling said to Counsel, 'You know the members of the Court of Appeal better than I do for I only see them in *church*,' and Counsel replies 'No doubt your Lordship sees them at their best', more often than not, Mr. Justice Darling is made to see them at *lunch*.

This book will make an excellent bed-book for it is a book to be tasted; but much of the pleasure will be in comparing the different versions that have come into being over the years, and to observe how the actors change from age to age. I very much hope that Mr. Jackson's industry will be rewarded by hosts of grateful readers.

INTRODUCTION

THIS book is intended to be neither exhaustive nor, one hopes, exhausting. In assembling my material on the lighter side of the Law I have had access to many works of biography and reminiscence, some long since out of print, and am grateful to the librarians of the Inner and Middle Temple for their patient co-operation and assistance.

To supplement these recorded anecdotes and witticisms, I tapped the memories of many barristers, solicitors and their clerks. The recollected treasure was rich and varied but often so confusing as partly to justify this volume.

Human memory, particularly when based on hearsay, is fallible. Some of the best legal stories have gone the long rounds and gathered dust. Frequently they are attributed to a great many different people. I have done all possible to check sources, and several pleasant witticisms have had to be discharged for lack of supporting evidence.

It has been tempting to use quips that border on the apocryphal, like the story of the advocate in the far north of Norway who asked a witness: 'Where were you on the night of 1st November to 28th March?'

Alas, there is no proof that this was ever asked. Nor is there documentary support for another classic story about the Hanging Judge who allegedly wept only once in his life.

That was when he was taken to see 'The Beggar's Opera' and deplored that Macheath was given a reprieve!

Much similar material has had to be rejected. On the other hand, I hope lawyers will forgive me for salvaging a few well-known stories which may still be appreciated by a younger generation and also by laymen in search of after-dinner anecdotes.

I have limited myself to the Courts of Great Britain and Eire. American and Continental lawyers and witnesses deserve separate treatment.

It will be noticed that stories of contemporary times are outnumbered by those from the Victorian and Edwardian days. 'Laughter in Court' is far less common than in the past when pugnacious advocacy and a lick of greasepaint were the fashion.

Today, more civil actions are tried without juries, and the somewhat unromantic County Courts are also handling a greater volume of cases. Expensive litigation has become a luxury and much is settled out of Court which would once have made rich public entertainment.

The whole atmosphere of the Courts has, of course, changed. Business is now handled more crisply and less dramatically. Advocates are much more restrained and Judges have for the most part stopped making witticisms which used to earn deferential, if not always deserved, applause.

The modern slump in legal wit and humour is partly due to the change in personnel at the Bar and inevitably on the Bench. Gone, perhaps forever, are the days when the sons of rich fathers gaily faced years of elegant unemployment as juniors and 'devils'. Today, of the 2,000 practising members of the English Bar only a handful can expect to earn anything approaching the vast, and far less taxable, incomes of 'the golden age'.

Bright young men are seeking higher rewards in the business world than at the overcrowded and underpaid Bar. And even legal giants like Monckton and Shawcross have strayed to the lusher and more easeful pastures of Industry and Banking.

Professional standards are far higher than in the past when port-flushed advocates were so often offensive to Judges and witnesses, and some members of the Bench delighted in brutal wit. Life on Circuit was also much more convivial, and good table talk helped to sharpen the wits.

In these days of donnish, rather earnest advocacy and a workmanlike Bench it may be amusing to recall some of the warriors in wigs who brought so much dash and colour to the solemn business of the Courts.

For connoisseurs and collectors of legal wit anxious for further reading, I would recommend Lord Darling's *Scintillal Juris* and that old classic, *Law and Laughter* by Morton and Malloch. Earthy, and often unconscious, humour is also provided by Police and County Court proceedings but, alas, daily newspaper reports are not as full as they were of old.

PART ONE

The Bench

The Bench

SIR FRANK LOCKWOOD irreverently described their lordships as looking 'like owls surveying a dead mouse in an
advanced stage of decomposition'. A kindlier definition was
once given by a guide who was showing some tourists
round the Law Courts.

'A Judge,' he said solemnly, 'is only a barrister who is
invited to sit on the Bench when he has had a lot of standing
at the Bar.'

⚏ ⚏ ⚏

With certain notable exceptions, particularly those who
flourished in the reign of good Queen Victoria, most
modern Judges have acknowledged that they are of human
clay.

After his first case, Mr. Justice Megaw recently confessed:
'I feel rather like a second-row forward who is suddenly
pulled out of the scrum, given a whistle and asked to
referee.' His learned brother-Judge, Mr. Justice Vaisey,
takes a view of the judicial office which few laymen—and
certainly few barristers—would dispute. 'Being a Judge is

17

the best career in the world,' he has said, semi-seriously. 'One is never contradicted, one is never interrupted, and one always has the last word.'

It is a sad reflection on human nature that Judges who are themselves verbose are usually the most inclined to be impatient of long-winded Counsel and tongue-tied witnesses.

Modern Judges are much less talkative and less inclined to interrupt than their predecessors. On his first day in Court, one new Judge put a little card in front of him on the Bench. It read simply, 'Shut up!'

At the end of the day he asked an old friend how he had fared.

'You will do very well if you learn to keep quiet,' said the barrister rather cuttingly.

　　　　　田　　　田　　　田

Before condemning their lordships for their occasional loss of patience, one must offer sympathy for the wear and tear on judicial nerves when assaulted by flatulence and the irrelevant.

In an action for false imprisonment, Counsel just kept rolling along like Ole Man River, repeating himself, almost but not quite, to a standstill. Finally, Mr. Justice Wightman leaned forward wearily.

'You've said that before,' he sighed.

'Have I, my lord?' mumbled Counsel. 'I'm very sorry. I quite forgot it.'

'Don't apologize,' said the wise and long-suffering old man. 'I forgive you, for it was a very long time ago.'

※ ※ ※

That great Scottish Judge, Lord Cockburn, had been kept late in Court, thanks to an advocate suffering from verbal dysentery. As he took off his lordship's heavy robes, his Clerk whispered sympathetically, 'Counsel has encroached very much on your time, my lord.'

'Time?' echoed Cockburn. 'He has exhausted time and encroached on eternity.'

※ ※ ※

On a very hot day, a man was being tried for stealing a ham, the main exhibit, which was beginning to wilt in the stuffy Court. Lord Bramwell summed up with commendable brevity.

'There, gentlemen of the jury, is the prisoner, and there, gentlemen, is the ham. Consider your verdict.'

※ ※ ※

The same Judge was trying a farmer accused of shooting at a boy who was stealing his apples. Defence Counsel had plodded on valiantly for some time without noticing, apparently, that his lordship kept raising his eyes to heaven or to the Court clock; perhaps to both.

Finally, it had to grind to an end. The Judge proceeded

to make one of the tersest summings-up in legal history. Turning squarely to the jury, he said: 'I shall leave the case to you in eight words. The prisoner aimed at nothing and missed it.'

⊞ ⊞ ⊞

Bramwell once found himself confronted by a prisoner who had an even keener taste for brevity. His lordship was proceeding to pass sentence when the man in the dock broke in harshly with the pointed question, 'How much?'

'Three years,' said the Judge, crisply.

⊞ ⊞ ⊞

Lord Hewart, himself a former Press reporter, never lost the virtue of talking to the point and keeping it short and sharp. After hearing a tedious argument, he delivered judgment as follows:

'Counsel for the appellant has raised six points in support of this appeal. In the first point there is nothing, and the same applies to the others. Five times nothing are nothing. The appeal is dismissed!'

In another case he crushed a prosy barrister with a swift blow to his oratorical solar plexus.

'You seem to be inviting us to embark upon a sea which has no shore.'

⊞ ⊞ ⊞

Commenting on the complexities of the Shops (Sunday) Trading Restriction) Act of 1936, Section 2, Lord Hewart observed acidly:

'It might be possible, but I doubt if it would be easy, to compress in the same number of lines more fertile opportunities for doubt and error.'

But this chubby little man who could be so dour as L.C.J. was a different man away from the Courts. One night at the Savage Club it was his duty to propose the health of the guest of honour, a celebrated concert pianist. He did so like this:

'It is now my duty to sentence Brother Savage Moiseiwitsch to fifteen minutes' hard labour, during which he will execute Wagner and Liszt.'

Mr. Justice Avory was nicknamed 'The Acid Drop' and never made a joke while he was on the Bench. Smallish, with a long upper-lip and sideboards that stressed the craggy austerity of his face, he was a delight to the caricaturists if not to those members of the underworld who had the misfortune to appear before him.

White-faced, unblinking and never moving a muscle, he was as impassive as the figure of frozen justice on top of the Old Bailey. Never allowing himself the faintest hint of levity, he sternly snuffed out any attempt by Counsel to lighten the grim atmosphere.

Typical of his sarcasm—which nevertheless was always relevant to the business in hand—was an exchange with Counsel during an appeal against an assessment for rates.

The appellant, a former stockbroker, claimed that his property was now agricultural as he had bought some cattle and poultry. Avory pursed sour lips.

'What did you say your client was?' he asked Counsel.

'A retired stockbroker, my lord.'

'Well,' commented the Judge dryly, 'perhaps it would have been more fortunate if he had stocked his land with bulls and bears.'

　　　　　꩜　　꩜　　꩜

At one trial, after hearing Counsel's closing speeches, Avory's trimmed mouth moved barely a fraction as he began his summing-up. At this point, a little girl sitting in the gallery with her father, screamed, 'Daddy, Daddy, it's *alive.*'

During his days at the Bar, Avory sometimes indulged in biting sarcasm which made everyone laugh except, of course, the hapless victim. In the course of the marathon Druce-Portland case, he cross-examined a witness who said he had come from New York to be treated for a skin disease by Sir Morell Mackenzie who had introduced him to the Duke of Portland.

'Are you aware that Sir Morell was then only seventeen or eighteen years of age?' asked Avory.

'I don't mean to say I saw Sir Morell Mackenzie then,' protested the witness. 'I carried my letter of recommendation about with me for years before presenting it.'

'Waiting for him to grow up, I suppose?' suggested Counsel.

⊞   ⊞   ⊞

Another witness was a trifle vague about the date of his marriage. Shown the certificate, he said, 'Well, I was a bit out—a year, that's all.'

'That's all!' exclaimed Horace Avory. 'I beg your pardon, that is not all. You may be *in* for a year.'

⊞   ⊞   ⊞

But even Homer nods sometimes. Mr. Justice Avory was quizzing a witness with his usual severity.

'Let me see, you have been convicted before, haven't you?'

'Yes, sir, but it was due to the incapacity of my Counsel rather than to any fault of my own.'

'It always is,' smiled the Judge, 'and you have my sincere sympathy.'

'And I deserve it,' agreed the man, 'seeing that you were my Counsel on that occasion.'

⊞   ⊞   ⊞

In another case, opposing Counsel had cited a text from the Book of Job.

'That evidence is not admissible,' said Avory coldly, 'since you cannot put Job in the box.'

﹆﹆﹆

Mr. Justice Stephen, another severe Judge, disliked any flippancy. Nobody dared to smile, let alone laugh, without risking a severe reproof from the embalmed figure.

During one trial, a spectator in the public gallery was heard to guffaw at some amusing piece of evidence. The Judge had the culprit brought down at once, sternly reprimanded him and ordered him to stand beside the prisoner in the dock until the trial was over.

This Judge was an outstanding writer on legal subjects but far from impressive in Court either in learning or in his manner. Often he took refuge in sarcasm to impress his authority.

Counsel had accepted a much-needed 'dock brief' in a case of obtaining money by false pretences. Slowly he toiled on, trying to make bricks with precious little straw. He received no help from the stiff figure on the Bench.

Finally, Mr. Justice Stephen rested his massive head on his hands and opened his summing-up:

'According to his own Counsel, the prisoner is a great rascal. When I have reviewed the evidence to you, I think, gentlemen of the jury, you will be of the opinion that the accused is even more of a consummate scoundrel than his advocate has depicted.'

When this Judge retired, the occasion was marked by the usual flowery and rather tiresome expressions of regret from Q.C.s present. A fellow-Judge, almost comatose from boredom, whispered to one of his brethren:

'May there be no moaning at the Bar when I put out to sea.'

♟   ♟   ♟

Quite different was Lord Darling who notoriously played to the gallery. Douglas Hogg, later Lord Chancellor Hailsham, once said that Darling had demonstrated that to be wise it was not absolutely necessary to be dull, but his lordship often achieved tedium in his strenuous efforts to avoid it.

No other Judge has ever equalled his wit and flair for repartee, but one suspects that his more literary quips were cooked over the midnight oil and served fresh and piping hot in Court next morning.

Rather unkindly caricatured as wearing a cap and bells on the Bench, Darling was nevertheless a fine lawyer whose judgments, however waggishly delivered, were rarely reversed on Appeal.

He could be cynical. In the Court of Criminal Appeal, Counsel pleaded that, apart from this one crime—a slight case of murder—the appellant had an unblemished reputation.

'Unfortunately,' said his lordship, 'I have had to sentence to death too many persons who bore the highest character to enable me to give that argument more than its due weight.'

⊞ ⊞ ⊞

Irony was his liveliest weapon. Counsel had asked for a three months' adjournment to have certain German documents translated.

'Why three months?' asked Darling.

'Because the documents which require translation are so technical,' explained Counsel.

'Rather a good idea has occurred to me,' said the Judge thoughtfully. 'Why not go to someone who knows German already?'

⊞ ⊞ ⊞

A keen horseman, the Judge enjoyed himself in a libel action brought by Richard Wootton, the trainer, against a racing newspaper. There were scores of Turf celebrities in Court and Lord Lonsdale, one of the witnesses, asked to be called quickly as he wished to get away to Sandown where he was a Steward.

Darling shook his head. 'I understood that, as everybody was engaged here, there was to be no meeting today.'

Another witness, a jockey, had been sharply cross-examined and was almost out of the witness-box before his Counsel could re-examine him.

'Wait a minute,' smiled the Judge. 'Mr. Smith has not weighed-in yet.'

A stickler for the old-fashioned, the Judge did not like the new style of riding with short stirrups. He soon found a chance to air his views.

When Counsel mentioned that a jockey was paid only £15 to ride 'over the sticks', Darling frowned.

'They will cross the other Styx if they continue to ride with short leathers.'

𝇋   𝇋   𝇋

Darling had a finely developed palate for judicial cruelty. Pleading before him was a barrister who lacked some of his learned friends' social and cultural advantages. In moments of stress he always found trouble over his aitches which he dropped liberally all over the Court.

'Gentlemen of the jury,' he began solemnly, 'This is a simple charge of 'orse-stealing. The 'orse was stolen by somebody and the 'ole point for you to decide is whether it was done by the prisoner. Now the little 'orse was in 'is loose-box at 'alf-past two . . .'

'Mr.——' interrupted the Judge, 'to obviate all further difficulty, why not call it a pony?'

𝇋   𝇋   𝇋

Henry Duke (later Lord Merrivale, President of the Probate, Divorce and Admiralty Division) was appearing before Darling in a dispute over a singer's ability to appear in a certain opera.

'He doesn't sing like the Archangel Gabriel,' admitted an expert witness.

'I have never heard the Archangel Gabriel sing,' commented Counsel with heavy sarcasm.

'That is a pleasure yet to come, Mr. Duke,' said the Judge.

Nobody enjoyed a cross-talk act with Counsel more than Darling, even if he came off second best.

A barrister had referred to the famous music-hall, the Coliseum, and his lordship could not resist his cue.

'Isn't that the place where the Christians feed the lions?' he asked innocently.

Mr. Vachell, K.C., shook his head gravely.

'I think your lordship must be thinking of the Trocadero where Lyons feed the Christians.'

Counsel had submitted that there was no case to go to the jury. Mr. Justice Darling was at his most urbane.

'If I withdraw it, Mr. Salter, may not the Court of Appeal say that I was wrong?'

Counsel smiled respectfully. 'I don't think your lordship need have anything to fear in this case from the Judges in the Court of Appeal.'

'Well, you know them better than I do,' said Darling. 'I only see them at church.'

'I feel sure that your lordship sees them at their best,' commented Counsel.

♙   ♙   ♙

Like so many other Judges of the old school he had a weakness for what is known as 'judicial ignorance', an irritating pose that modern Judges have happily abandoned.

'And who is George Robey?' he asked during one action.

Counsel returned the ball neatly.

'He is the Darling of the music-halls, my lord.'

♙   ♙   ♙

Lord Coleridge also liked to profess ignorance. Mr. Dewar was cross-examining a witness.

'What was your condition at the time?'

'Well, I'd just had a nip.'

'A nip?' echoed the Judge. 'What is a nip?'

'Only a small Dewar,' explained the witness.

♙   ♙   ♙

Coleridge, silver-tongued and learned, had a neat turn of phrase. During a technical case of copyright, he remarked:

'Even in music there is variety of opinion. Some love their Bach often, while others prefer their Offenbach.'

♙   ♙   ♙

Lord Esher, a handsome and dandified figure for an old Cambridge rowing Blue, was something of a terror on the Bench. Junior members of the Bar became nervous wrecks in front of him and sometimes forgot their 'lines' like amateurs on a first night.

During one breach of promise action he began his usual tactics of harrying the young barrister who appeared for the plaintiff. Counsel argued seriously and at length that the defendant had taken the injured lady to look over a house. This, he pleaded, was surely evidence that he had proposed marriage.

'That's no corroboration,' said the Judge testily. 'Do you not know that gentlemen take houses for their mistresses?'

'I was not aware of it,' said the young man.

'I can hardly believe that,' laughed the Judge, 'but you can take it from me that they do.'

'I bow to your lordship's superior knowledge,' said Counsel.

ꕤ   ꕤ   ꕤ

This same Judge could be most soft-spoken and courtly to the ladies who were not usually slow in flattering him. A certain woman was a notorious litigant and a nuisance to most Judges. Her policy was to object to their lordships, usually in the most offensive terms, but she could not resist Lord Esher who presided over the Court of Appeal.

He addressed her in his most winning style.

'Last time you came here, you complained that your case had been tried by my brother Bowen, who was only a

31

2

bit of a boy and could not do you justice. Now you come here and say that my brother Bacon was too old.' He sighed. 'What age do you want the Judge to be?'

'Your age,' said the appellant meltingly.

　　　Ⓜ　　　Ⓜ　　　Ⓜ

On at least one occasion Lord Esher misfired with this gallantry. He was hearing a complicated action concerning shares in a gold-mine. The plaintiff, an elderly lady, was receiving the familiar kid-gloved treatment from the Judge who was in jocular vein.

When Counsel mentioned a mine known as 'Moaning Flat', his lordship laughed, 'That sounds like the name of some place below.'

The lady turned a severe glance upon him. 'It ill becomes a white-haired old man like you, my lord, to be profane.'

This rebuke caused such hilarity among the Press reporters that one of them nearly choked and had to be assisted from the Court. For days afterwards, the Judge's manner showed no distinction between the sexes.

He retired at the age of eighty-two and gracefully thanked the Bar for their good wishes which were sincere, although many had smarted under his tongue.

'I think I could have gone on a little longer,' he said wistfully, 'but I thought it right, considering my age, that there should be a period of absolute rest in order to prepare for the next stage.'

　　　Ⓜ　　　Ⓜ　　　Ⓜ

The Lord Advocate was addressing the Court in Edinburgh.

'Suppose, for example, milord, I were to see you going into a public house . . .'

'Coming,' corrected the Judge with a smile.

※　　※　　※

During a murder trial, the prisoner whispered something to the policeman who sat beside him in the dock. Counsel for the prosecution at once demanded that the constable should reveal what was said to him.

The P.C. squirmed. Counsel bullied. The Judge approved.

'Constable,' said Mr. Justice Hawkins sternly, 'Inform the Court what passed between you and the prisoner.'

'I would rather not, your lordship.'

Hawkins bared his teeth like a bulldog. 'Never mind what you would rather not do,' he snapped. 'Inform the Court at once what the prisoner said.'

The constable tried to keep his voice steady.

'He asked me, your lordship, who that hoary heathen with the sheepskin was, as he had often seen him on the racecourse.'

※　　※　　※

Hawkins liked nothing better than to rush through his cases, particularly if he wanted to get away to attend a race-meeting or some other social event. In the stifling atmosphere which he encouraged by never allowing a window in Court to be opened, he bestowed his affection entirely upon his favourite dog, Jack, who sat with him on the Bench.

On a certain occasion, and one very rare for this well-trained animal, Jack was guilty of 'barking in Court'. Hawkins shot a fierce glance at the gallery and said:

'Order that dog out!' Meanwhile, he stroked and quietened the animal snuggling under his robes.

♙ ♙ ♙

This same Judge usually showed far more tolerance to witnesses than he did to members of the Bar, but he was becoming quite purple with impatience at Counsel's efforts to keep a voluble old lady on the rails of logic. Finally, he stepped in and asked a blunt question.

The witness rounded on him. 'It's no use bothering me,' she snapped at the Bench. 'I've told you all I know.'

'That may be,' agreed his lordship soothingly, 'but the question rather is, do you know all you have told us?'

♙ ♙ ♙

Mr. Justice Humphreys was one of the greatest of our criminal judges. He was also blessed with the gift of commonsense.

At Birmingham Assizes he listened impatiently to a police witness who said that the road 'staggered' near a public house.

Sir Travers gave a judicial snort.

'I can quite understand that people who come out of a public house stagger, but I can't see how a road can stagger. Do you mean it curves? Everything seems to stagger these

34

days. Holidays are staggered; daylight is staggered; working hours are staggered; and now roads are being staggered.'

※　　　※　　　※

That very patient and amiable London magistrate, Mr. Cancellor, once found himself under cross-examination in his own Court. The accused was a docker charged with assault and Mr. Cancellor asked if he had anything to say before sentence was passed. This is a formal question usually received by a tearful plea for mercy or, quite often, a sharp obscenity that denies the jurisdiction of the Court or the paternity of the magistrate.

Not so in this particular case. The prisoner turned to the Bench with complete self-possession.

'Supposing you had been working hard all the week. I ask you to suppose that.' Mr. Cancellor nodded.

'Suppose you got out of bed on a Sunday morning and wanted to look a bit decent like.' Mr. Cancellor supposed.

'Suppose you had only one decent pair of trousers.' Mr. Cancellor was prepared to accept the possibility.

'Suppose you found your missus had pawned your only decent pair of trousers.' Mr. Cancellor tried to imagine that Mrs. Cancellor had committed this act of treachery.

Prisoner (triumphantly): 'What would *you* do to your missus then? You would do what I did—you would 'it her.'

Mr. Cancellor collected himself and tried to keep a straight face. 'You are discharged today,' he said quietly, 'but don't use the frying-pan next time.'

36

The Judge once discovered, however, that being too literal could also prove dangerous. During his days as Treasury Counsel he had prosecuted Dr. Crippen and this was recalled in an interview when he visited New York.

'You the man who hanged Crippen?' he was asked.

'No, the jury convicted him.'

'Do you regard English Law as superior to ours?'

'I'm afraid I don't know American Law so I cannot express an opinion,' he answered amiably enough.

Next morning the headlines read:

'Man who hanged Crippen says he knows no law!'

◫   ◫   ◫

Some Judges have taken pains to disparage the jury system. Not so Sir Travers Humphreys who had a very soft spot for those he liked to call 'The Great Unpaid'.

'I cannot understand,' he once said, 'why it is thought that justice in this country can be better administered by making jurors and witnesses as uncomfortable as possible. They are worse off than prisoners who in the dock have plenty of room.'

◫   ◫   ◫

Another London 'Beak' had a sharp nose for the eloquent scamps who sometimes appeared before him.

The accused was asked if he pleaded guilty or not guilty to the charge of being drunk. Silver-haired and with the dignity of a bishop, the man replied earnestly, 'Not guilty, sir. I was certainly not drunk, though I may have been intoxicated.'

The magistrate nodded understandingly. 'I had intended to fine you ten shillings but, in the light of your explanation, I shall make it half a sovereign.'

⚏   ⚏   ⚏

Judge Cluer had his own methods of dealing with witnesses who were a little careless in handling the truth.

In one case he was listening impatiently to a witness who was spinning some very tall stories indeed. Finally, His Honour decided to intervene.

'Just you look around the Court,' he said sternly. 'You will notice there are seven doors to it. Now, if you go on lying like this, I will have you cut in seven pieces and each piece shall be carried through a separate door.'

The witness snatched up his hat and dashed from the Court like a greyhound after a toy rabbit.

⚏   ⚏   ⚏

At Marylebone Police Court, the magistrate used to be Mr. Broderip, who was also an F.Z.S. and prided himself on his scientific knowledge.

In one case over an affiliation order, Counsel for the

2*

defendant argued strenuously that his client could not have been the father. Mr. Broderip thought otherwise and granted the application.

Before he rose he courteously called the barrister over for a few words.

'You made a very good speech,' he said pleasantly, 'and I was inclined to decide in your favour, but you know I am a bit of a naturalist. While you were speaking I was comparing the child with your client, and there could be no mistake. The likeness was most striking.'

'Good heavens!' exclaimed the barrister. 'My client was not in Court. The man you saw was my clerk.'

♙　　♙　　♙

At West London, that popular magistrate, Sir Gervais Rentoul, had to settle a dispute between two women neighbours who lived in the same house and always quarrelled. The climax came when one of the ladies apparently broke into the other's room and amused herself by playing on a piano of which the owner was very proud.

'Why, you haven't got a piano,' denied the other when the case came up in Court.

'I haven't *now*, but I can prove I had one. If you, sir,' (smiling at the magistrate), 'will come round to my place you will see the top of the piano in my room.'

'The *top* of your piano?' echoed Sir Gervais in some astonishment.

'Well, I was so furious at her playing it that I took the piano to bits.'

The magistrate could not believe his ears and asked for more details. 'I took out the notes and gave some to a friend next door and some to the woman across the street. They used them as firewood.'

Sir Gervais scratched a puzzled ear. 'Well, it couldn't have been very much of a piano,' he suggested.

'No, sir,' agreed the injured party. 'I got it second-hand and paid five shillings for it.'

The magistrate thought it was high time he passed on to the next case. He bound the two ladies over to keep the peace.

॥   ॥   ॥

County Court Judges rarely permit themselves the flatulence of their superior brethren on the Queen's Bench.

At Shoreditch the Judge listened impatiently to a long-winded defendant who ended on this note of passion:

'As the Lord is my judge, I do not owe this money.'

Snapped His Honour: 'He's not. I am. You do.'

॥   ॥   ॥

A man had been found guilty of felony and Mr. Justice Maule prepared to pass sentence.

'May God strike me dead, my lord, if I did it!' shouted the prisoner.

The Judge paused for a full minute in the silent Court. Then he intoned solemnly, 'As Providence has not seen fit to interpose in your case, it now becomes my duty to pronounce upon you the sentence of the Law . . .'

❏   ❏   ❏

The same Judge had before him a man who was asked if he wished to call any witnesses. He replied, 'None but my Maker, who is well aware of my complete innocence.'

His lordship turned to the jury and observed, 'Gentlemen, the prisoner is charged with stealing a watch. He calls a witness who does not appear. On the other hand, two witnesses saw him take the watch. Consider your verdict.'

❏   ❏   ❏

A fire-eating advocate of the old school showed no mercy to the unhappy witnesses opposing him. One elderly lady was so petrified that she temporarily lost the use of her tongue and could only turn piteously to the Bench, presided over by Mr. Justice Maule.

Counsel glowered at her and repeated his question. In vain she struggled for words.

'Why don't you answer?' asked the Judge.

'Because, my lord, he frightens me so.'

'So he does me, ma'am,' clucked his lordship sympathetically.

❏   ❏   ❏

This Judge could also be withering. Counsel had meandered through his brief in a most confused and confusing fashion. When it appeared that he was chasing a will-o'-the-wisp round an endless maze, his lordship had to intervene.

'Mr. Barker, cannot you state your facts in some kind of order? Chronological is the best but, if you can't manage that, try *some* order. Why not alphabetical?'

◫   ◫   ◫

The advocate of yesterday often aimed at eloquence and only hit flatulence. A woman was charged before Mr. Justice Byles with having caused the death of her child by depriving it of proper food and care.

Counsel pulled out all the stops in addressing the jury. 'Gentlemen, it appears to be impossible that the prisoner could have committed this crime. A mother guilty of such conduct to her own child? Why, it is repugnant to our better feelings.'

With gestures worthy of Irving or Martin Harvey, he continued tremulously, 'Gentlemen, the beasts of the field, the birds of the air, suckle their young . . .'

This was really too much for his lordship who broke in sharply: 'If you establish the latter part of your proposition, your client will undoubtedly be acquitted.'

◫   ◫   ◫

Richard Webster, later Lord Chief Justice Alverstone, had

been a great all-round athlete in his youth and liked to box a few rounds even in middle-age.

One day he was presiding over a trial during which defence Counsel kept trying to demonstrate the difference between a real and a sham threat. The Judge became so bored that he leaned forward and said to this barrister:

'Mr. Jones, just deal with this point. Suppose I threatened to punch your head unless you sat down. Would that be a real or a sham threat?'

Counsel did not hesitate. 'A sham, my lord,' he said brightly. 'All the world knows that Dick Webster would never hit a man smaller than himself!'

◩   ◩   ◩

In later years a little hard of hearing, the kindly old L.C.J. always tried to make sure that he did not miss any of the evidence. He was anxious to be particularly helpful to a man who was defending himself on a serious charge.

At one point the Judge cupped his ear. 'What was your last sentence?' he asked the accused.

'Six months,' came the prompt reply.

◩   ◩   ◩

Lord Alverstone showed great humanity after sentencing a young playboy and gambler to nine months in gaol. He was saddened that a youth of good family and education should find himself disgraced and, on sudden impulse, arranged for him to be brought to his private room before being taken to prison.

'You have real abilities,' said the Judge warmly. 'Why don't you settle down and make good?'

'How much do you make in your present job?' asked the young man coolly.

'The State gives me £8,000 a year.'

'I make twice that already,' the prisoner said loftily.

🔖 🔖 🔖

In his more relaxed moments, Lord Alverstone enjoyed telling his cronies a story against himself. He used to sing in the choir at his local parish church and, one Sunday, a tourist went there expressly to see the Lord Chief Justice.

Slipping the verger a florin she begged him to point out the famous lawyer.

'Well, ma'am,' said the verger, 'it's like this. There's me and the vicar. As for the choir, so long as they behave themselves, we don't inquire too closely about their past.'

🔖 🔖 🔖

Mr. Justice Wright left Court early one morning and by 11 a.m. was comfortably tucked into an armchair at his club, sheltered by *The Times*. In walked his brother-Judge, Bowen, who greeted him cheerily, 'Hello, having a day off?'

'Not at all,' returned Wright with some asperity. 'I have

finished my List for the day. I have tried six Non-Jury Actions.'

'Oh,' said Bowen. 'Well, my advice to you is: go back to Court and hear the other side.'

❊   ❊   ❊

Guilty of unconscious humour was a magistrate who presided at the Hertfordshire Sessions. A rather pompous barrister named Thomas had certain local associations with the town and in his opening made a flowery speech in which he said what great pleasure it gave him to revisit a place of which he had such happy memories, and so on. . . .

His flow of irrelevant reminiscences was checked by a man from the gallery who shouted rudely, 'Bosh, Tommy, bosh!'

Counsel protested angrily and the Chairman was moved to support him in terms which were a little unfortunate.

'I quite agree, Mr. Thomas,' he said warmly, 'and the interruption was both uncalled-for and ill-timed. I hope for the rest of the proceedings that nobody will say "Bosh!" until he has heard both sides.'

❊   ❊   ❊

Mr. Commissioner Kerr, presiding over a City of London Bench, listened patiently to a series of witnesses who contradicted themselves and each other with a quite alarming contempt for the risk of perjury.

46

He began his summing-up: 'David said in his haste, all men are liars. If he were sitting in this Court, he would have said the same thing at his leisure.'

⊞   ⊞   ⊞

Mr. Justice Langton was hearing a petition for divorce on the grounds of nullity, brought by a young wife against her elderly husband.

As usual, in a defended action, much depends on the demeanour of the parties and the impression they make in the witness-box.

In this case, the Judge had clearly paid great attention to the manner in which the parties had given their evidence and he expressed his view with gentle but perceptive irony.

'I greatly prefer the younger, fresher and far clearer memory of the petitioner to the fuddled recollection of the respondent. His idea of giving evidence is to say first whatever he chooses to say at the moment, and then to prune it down as recollection returns to him and reminds him of the true facts.'

⊞   ⊞   ⊞

In the Scottish Courts a youth was charged with stealing from a chemist's shop.

'Weel, ye see, I had a bit o' pain in me side and my mother tauld me to gang to the chemist's and take something.'

'Oh, yes, of course,' conceded the Judge, 'but surely she didn't tell you to go and take an eight-day clock.'

♙   ♙   ♙

Lord Justice Asquith once confessed honestly that he was puzzled over the tortured horrors of the Rent Restriction Acts.

'I yield to them the reluctant respect one feels for an old tough sparring partner whom one has never been able to knock out.'

♙   ♙   ♙

Judges vary in their methods of expounding wisdom. Some favour the rotund and oracular while not a few prefer the simple, homely analogy.

Lord Justice Sankey remarked to the jury during a summing-up: 'One recalls the instance of the lady who in a West End drawing-room accused a noble lord of being a thief. But she added that he had stolen her heart. You will agree that to call a person a thief is not necessarily actionable.'

♙   ♙   ♙

Lord Justice Knight Bruce had a taste for involved sarcasm. Discussing the marriage settlement of a certain naval captain, he delivered himself as follows:

'This litigation owes its origin to the manner in which

a series of professional gentlemen in the north of England permitted themselves to transact, or in more accurate phrase to entangle or perplex, some legal business entrusted to their care.

'These licensed pilots undertook to steer a captain through certain not very narrow straits of the Law, and with abundance of sea room ran him aground on every sea shoal that they could make.'

      ⊞   ⊞   ⊞

Mr. Justice Mathew could be very cutting. 'Can you tell me what kind of a bird this is?' a witness demanded brusquely.

'Well, my friend,' said the Judge, 'if there is any truth in the adage that birds of a feather flock together, I should say it was a gaolbird.'

      ⊞   ⊞   ⊞

This Judge often dropped an aside which only sharp-eared Counsel could catch. With half-closed eyes, Mathew was once heard to mutter: 'Truth will out, even in an affidavit.'

      ⊞   ⊞   ⊞

Mr. Justice Blackburn also had a rough tongue. Two men before him were charged with committing a felony. They were acquitted. As they stepped with relief from the dock, one of them turned to the other and said: 'How that Judge did bully our counsellor!'

'He did, George, he did, but he were fair. He bullied that persecuting chap just as much.'

♙   ♙   ♙

Mr. Justice Boyd was short and sharp with those who sought jury exemption on flimsy grounds.

'My lord, 'tis a great hardship on me,' pleaded one ancient.

'It's a great hardship on myself but I attend here and do my duty,' said the Judge.

'And I'm old.'

'I'm certain you're ten years younger than myself.'

'And, my lord, I'm getting deaf.'

'I'm deaf myself but I manage to hear enough to do justice,' said his lordship grimly.

'And I'm so stupid, my lord.'

'I'm just as——'. The Judge stopped himself in time. 'No more nonsense, man. You've got to serve.'

♙   ♙   ♙

It is always reported of this Judge that, throughout his career on the Bench, he sipped his port through a specially made tube like a penholder which fitted into a metal inkstand filled with his favourite vintage.

During one trial the witness stoutly denied that he was intoxicated at the time of the alleged offence.

'Come now, my good man,' said Boyd testily, 'it is a very important consideration. Tell the Court truly were you drunk or were you sober upon that occasion?'

The witness looked fixedly at the Bench.

'Oh, quite sober, my lord. In fact, *as sober as a Judge*.'

Most Judges like to protect witnesses from Counsel's sarcasm. During an involved farming dispute, one of the experts was being roughly handled in cross-examination.

'You are the clerk of the market and have been for thirty years?' asked Counsel with a faint air of surprise.

'Yes, and my father before me.'

'Never mind your father!' snapped Counsel.

The Judge leaned forward with a smile. 'He means, Mr. ——, that though his pedigree does not interest you, it is of consequence to him.'

Mr. Justice Walton employed quite another method with a barrister who was making a strenuous appeal to sentiment. The Judge had just sentenced a man to seven years' penal servitude for a most serious offence when the advocate jumped up and pleaded passionately that the prisoner's health was very poor.

'My client cannot live out half that term and I beg you to change the sentence,' he said in vibrant tones.

The Judge nodded. 'In that case, if you prefer, I will make it for life instead of seven years.'

Counsel quickly agreed that the original sentence would be *quite* satisfactory, and his delicate client would be pleased to take his chance of survival.

🙣　🙣　🙣

The hectoring style of advocacy was condemned once and for all by Baron Alderson. Counsel had been handling his brief like a knuckle-duster when the Judge interposed: 'Mr. ——, you seem to think that the art of cross-examination is to examine crossly.'

🙣　🙣　🙣

Alderson had to try a man clearly guilty of having stolen a pair of shoes. He had decided not to brief Counsel and this made the Judge even more anxious to be helpful.

'Do tell the jury exactly what happened,' he said in a kindly tone.

The man shuffled uncomfortably in the shoes concerned.

'Well, my lord, it was like this,' he said conversationally. 'I saw the shoes on a stall outside the shop and thought I might have a bit of fun with the chap who owned the shop. As soon as his back was turned, I just leaned over and took 'em.'

'So it was only a practical joke?' murmured the Judge.

'Yes, it was,' agreed the accused eagerly.

'And how far did you carry the shoes?'

'A matter of a couple of miles, my lord.'

Alderson turned to the jury. 'I think that is carrying the joke too far, don't you?'

⊞   ⊞   ⊞

Judges are always helpful to nervous witnesses of tender years and rightly severe with advocates who try to trap the unwary and inexperienced. One Judge was patiently trying to find out if a young lad really understood the nature of the oath.

'Now, my little man,' he said gently, 'do you know what will become of you if you tell an untruth?'

'Hell fire,' said the boy readily.

'Well, and what will become of you if you play truant and do not go to school?'

'Hell fire.'

'What if you stay out late when your mother sends you on an errand?'

'Hell fire.'

And so the catechism went on, with always the same emphatic and inevitable reply to each of the Judge's questions.

Finally, Counsel on the other side thought fit to intervene.

'My lord, I hardly think this little boy sufficiently intelligent or instructed for his evidence to be admissible.'

'Nonsense!' barked his lordship. 'I entirely differ from you. He seems a very good little boy and, if he grows up in his present belief and thinks the direst punishment will be visited upon him for every fault he may commit, he will probably make a much better man than you or I.'

The boy was duly sworn.

⊞   ⊞   ⊞

The young witness can sometimes prove anything but an asset. A scrap of a girl stepped daintily into the box during a County Court case and was greeted with a friendly smile from the Bench.

'How old are you?' asked His Honour.

'Ten, sir.'

'And do you understand what an oath is?'

'Oh, yes, it's what father uses when he falls over the cat.'

'And do you know what will happen if you do not tell the truth in this Court?'

'Yes, sir. Our side will win.'

⊞   ⊞   ⊞

Mr. Justice Day was always most slovenly dressed and rather absent in his manner. He had little patience with Counsel and was particularly irritated when he was accosted, as he was leaving his Court, by a newly-called young barrister whose family he knew slightly.

'I'm thinking of joining a Circuit,' confided the young man.

'Oh, do,' growled the Judge, sweeping on. 'Join the South-Eastern Circuit and stop at Colney Hatch.'

⊞   ⊞   ⊞

In a libel action before the same Judge one of the witnesses was an undertaker who, on being asked his name and address, produced his business card from force of habit.

Glancing at it Counsel asked, in some surprise, 'Why do you include your telegraphic address?'

'Oh,' put in Mr. Justice Day, 'I suppose it is for the convenience of people who want to be buried in a hurry.'

❦ ❦ ❦

Mr. Justice Lawrance was smooth of manner but sly in wit. In sentencing a prisoner he referred to him as 'a professional burglar'.

The man protested violently from the dock. 'I dunno what you mean! Professional! I've only done it once before, and I've been nabbed both times.'

The Judge gave him a cool smile. 'Oh, I didn't mean to say that you had been very *successful* in your profession.'

❦ ❦ ❦

At the Old Bailey, a man was accused of being in possession of housebreaking implements; to wit, a jemmy and screw-driver.

'They are the tools of my trade, my lord,' he protested indignantly.

'That is precisely what the prosecution alleges,' pointed out the Judge.

❦ ❦ ❦

Sir Henry Dickens, the Common Serjeant and son of the novelist, was about to sentence an old lag who barked:

'You ain't a patch on your dad!'

'I quite agree with you,' said the Judge amiably, 'but what do you know about my father?'

'Oh, I've read all 'is books.'

'Really? Where?'

'Well, I read some in prison.'

'Have you?' said Sir Henry, with a pleasant smile. 'That's capital, for you will now have eighteen months in which to resume your studies.'

🏵   🏵   🏵

On another occasion, a man asked his solicitor who the Judge was.

'Mr. Dickens, K.C., is the Commissioner of Assize. You know, the son of Charles Dickens.'

'Ah,' said his client, 'I seem to have heard that name before. Oh, yes, I've got it! Why, of course, it's that chap who writes the music-hall sketches for Bransby Williams.'

🏵   🏵   🏵

In the days when Judges were sometimes two-bottle men, one of the most convivial was Mr. Justice Manisty who dearly loved his port. His fine cellar was famous and he seemed determined to empty it before he passed on. This ambition was checked by his doctor who firmly ordered him off all intoxicating liquor.

His lordship languished and became so frail that the physician finally decided that he had better take to his port again.

'Aye, doctor,' said the Judge, 'but how about *the arrears?*'

ㅁ   ㅁ   ㅁ

Another Judge had a distressing experience in Munster. He summed-up rather pompously as follows.

'In order that you may understand the legal aspect of this case, it is necessary that I should explain to you as representing the merchant princes of this city the meaning and effect of a composition in bankruptcy.'

With some notable exceptions, the members of the jury burst into a roar of laughter which the Judge, who had intended a graceful compliment, did not appreciate.

It was tactfully explained to him later that the foreman and one or two fellow-jurymen had only recently filed their petitions in bankruptcy themselves.

ㅁ   ㅁ   ㅁ

Judge Morris had a voice that was the richest Dublin. He was in London attending the wedding of a fellow-Judge's daughter and turned to a barrister friend with a sentimental look.

'Ah,' he sighed, 'I wish I had brought a shoe to throw at them.'

'Never mind, old boy,' consoled his friend. 'Why not throw your brogue?'

A certain Judge, Gainsford Bruce, was such a great bore that Counsel fought hard to avoid the labour of appearing before him.

One day Frank Lockwood was leaving his Court with an old friend, Bosanquet, K.C., when he remarked sourly, 'Bosey, I think you are the dullest man I ever met.'

'Yes,' said Bosanquet good-humouredly, 'but have you seriously considered the case of his lordship?'

⊞　⊞　⊞

Baron Martin was so good-natured that he sometimes found it difficult to pass sentence. In one case of petty theft, he addressed the accused as follows: 'Look, I hardly know what to do with you, but you can take six months.'

The prisoner knew his man. 'I can't take that, my lord,' he wheedled. 'It's too much. Your lordship sees I did not steal very much after all.'

'Well, that's very true,' said the Judge. 'Well then, you can take four. Will that do?'

The man shook his head. 'No, I can't take that either.'

The Judge almost began to coax. 'Then take three.'

'That's nearer the mark, my lord, but I'd rather you'd make it *two*, if you'll be so kind.'

'Very well then,' sighed his lordship. 'Take two, and don't come again.' He tried to look severe. 'If you do, I'll give you—well, it'll all depend. . . .'

⊞　⊞　⊞

Martin had many virtues but these did not include an understanding of the arts. While on Circuit he had to try a case for which some knowledge of Shakespeare would not have been a disadvantage. In his lodgings, the night before, the Judge read *Romeo and Juliet* for the first time.

Next morning he observed to his Marshal.

'Well, I've read it and I find that it is a tissue of improbabilities from beginning to end.'

　　　　🁢　　🁢　　🁢

Judge Tudor Rees has recalled an occasion when the quality of mercy provided quite unexpected dividends. He had before him a man charged with obtaining money by false pretences.

From a sound family background and after a first-class education he had drifted into petty crime and been sent to prison. After that, like so many others, he had returned to his old ways because it had been difficult for a man with his record to find a job.

The Judge listened with sympathy and was impressed by the accused's frank manner. He therefore decided to impose a light sentence of six months.

'Fair enough,' said the man cheerfully. 'And don't forget Fickle Fanny for the 3.30 on Friday.'

Not a betting man normally, the Judge thanked him with a laugh. Later, however, he passed the 'tip' on to his Clerk. Together they looked up the form which was far from reassuring, but the Judge decided to risk a cautious fiver each way.

Fickle Fanny duly showed her respect for the Law by obliging at 25 to 1.

☙　☙　☙

Breach of promise actions, now happily on the decline, have often produced more hilarity than heartache in our Courts. Eros is apt to look a trifle absurd with an open quiverful of old love letters.

With his usual Lancashire commonsense and good humour, Mr. Justice Swift always enjoyed himself hearing these cases. In one action he summed up after hearing that the defendant had jilted the lady because of her alleged bad temper.

'The mere fact that a woman has a temper does not render her unfit for matrimony. Otherwise, half the population of this world would never have been born.'

In a similar case, Counsel had apologized for having made a mistake.

'To err is human . . .' he said winningly.

'But who am I to forgive?' countered the Judge, reaching for the bottle of smelling salts which he was always sniffing.

☙　☙　☙

Swift figured in an amusing incident during a divorce hearing. A maid gave her evidence, answering each question with an automatic 'yes'.

Counsel took her smoothly through the familiar details.

'You served them breakfast in bed?'

'Yes.'

'Is this a photograph of the co-respondent?'

'Yes.'

Counsel sat down quite satisfied but, alas, not for long.

'You haven't proved your case,' said his lordship sadly.

Counsel rose to his feet, amazed. 'With respect, I thought I had,' he protested.

His lordship shook his head with a smile. 'Ah, but you see, I inadvertently passed the wrong photograph to the witness. The one she identified was used in a previous case.'

ᛗ ᛗ ᛗ

In another divorce suit, Counsel for the respondent waxed eloquent on the subject of his client's fine war record. Mr. Justice Swift raised a finger of reproval.

'In my view, there is no consistency between gallantry on the battlefield and gallantry in the boudoir.'

ᛗ ᛗ ᛗ

Like most Judges, Swift J. was not over-fond of expert witnesses. One of them, a veterinary surgeon, kept mumbling his evidence until all his wisdom was being limited to himself exclusively.

'Do speak up,' snapped his lordship. 'Don't whisper as though you were giving us a tip from the horse's mouth.'

ᛗ ᛗ ᛗ

This respected Judge had a generous share of common humanity. He had his little weaknesses including a taste for a nip of whisky on a cold night.

Before him appeared a man charged with being drunk while driving home. Defending Counsel pleaded with passion that his client had only taken a small Scotch and soda on New Year's Eve and just one for the road after midnight.

Swift summed up briskly and with a twinkle in his eye.

'Now, what are the facts? Why, this man had one drink in 1933, and didn't have another until 1934.'

Verdict, 'Not Guilty'.

෴ ෴ ෴

He was not the kind of Judge to lose his temper even under provocation. A nervous young junior was obviously trying to conceal his inexperience under the armour of aggression. His manner was soon beginning to upset a woman witness who, like himself, was making her first appearance in a Court of Law.

'Now, look here, my good woman, you really must not keep addressing me as m'lud,' he said crossly.

At this point Mr. Justice Swift decided to intervene.

'You must not be angry with the witness,' he chided mildly. 'Perhaps, after all, it is only a little intelligent anticipation.'

෴ ෴ ෴

3

Counsel always knew when this Judge was becoming irritable. He would start tapping his pencil on the desk like a schoolmaster and the Bar usually took this as a danger signal and a warning.

Not so one determined barrister who was patiently hammering at a point, seemingly oblivious of the machine-gun rattle from the Bench.

'Really, Mr. Smith, where are we now?' at last demanded his lordship.

'About the middle of my cross-examination,' came the unruffled reply.

田   田   田

Mr. Justice Swift did not take cheerfully to the mechanical dreariness and squalor of divorce work.

'I suppose it is a very pleasant thing to commit adultery,' he once observed, 'but it becomes rather monotonous to listen to other people having done it, hour after hour and day after day.'

田   田   田

Mr. Justice Hill also shared his distaste for these judicial chores. When appointed to hear both Admiralty and Divorce actions, he remarked sadly, 'Now I have one foot in the sea and another in a sewer.'

田   田   田

That great crusading Judge and reformer, Mr. Justice

McCardie, was a lifelong bachelor. He was once driving to the Courts with a chatty cab-driver who asked if he was married. The Judge shook his head.

'I'm thinking of marrying a widow who's got her own cottage and a bit of money,' confided the cabby.

'Why don't you?' asked McCardie. 'Is she ugly?'

'Oh, no! She's a nice-looking woman but it's the family. You see, she has twelve children by her first man and she's still young enough to have some more.'

'Wouldn't you like to marry her?' asked the Judge, choking with laughter.

'Well,' said the man gravely, 'I might when she gets a bit older.'

♛   ♛   ♛

When he was appointed to the Bench, McCardie was entertained to dinner by a host of legal friends.

Smilingly he looked around him and observed: 'I am especially glad to see here tonight those hundred solicitors, each of whom sent me my first brief.'

♛   ♛   ♛

Probate has caused loss of fortune and rifts in friendship but sometimes it has helped to pierce the gloom of the Courts.

A former Master of the Rolls had, rather incredibly, left his fortune to pay off the National Debt. One of his old judicial colleagues, trying to decide the validity of the will, commented unkindly, 'He might as well have attempted to stop the middle arch of Blackfriars Bridge with his full-bottomed wig.'

The will was subsequently set aside because the testator was proved to have been somewhat adrift mentally when he drew it up.

♙ ♙ ♙

In another complicated action, Mr. Justice Eve remarked sorrowfully, 'I shudder to think that in the hereafter I shall have to meet those testators whose wishes on earth have been frustrated by my judgments.'

♙ ♙ ♙

It is notorious that many a lawyer has tripped over the simple formalities of drafting his own will and testament. But laymen, over-eager to save expense, are the worst offenders in this respect.

Giving judgment, Mr. Justice Harman once drew attention to this danger.

'The testator made his will by the expedient which so many testators adopt of buying a sixpenny or shilling form and filling it in. He then signed the will and no doubt thought he had done a good day's work as, for the legal profession, he had.'

♙ ♙ ♙

It is sad to have to record that one of the first editors of the classic *Jarman on Wills* died intestate!

♔　　♔　　♔

Most Judges, as we have suggested, like to get through their work without wasting time, but nothing irritates their lordships more than Counsel who are too obviously galloping ahead to suit their own personal convenience.

An advocate appearing for the defence in a claim for compensation seemed in some haste to get this case over and rush into the adjoining Court with another brief.

'Happy to say, m'lud,' he began breathlessly, 'no conflict over plaintiff's condition in this case.' He took a deep breath and charged on. 'Our doctors think he's going to get well. His own doctors think he's going to get well. His wife thinks he's going to get well. Plaintiff himself thinks he's going to get well. . . .'

The Judge smiled pleasantly. 'But *I* don't think he's going to get well.'

♔　　♔　　♔

Poor Mr. Justice Field was very deaf, which proved less of an affliction to himself than to those who had to plead before him.

One day a barrister opened his case only to be sharply interrupted by Hawkins, J. 'I will trouble you not to shout at me like that,' he barked.

'I beg your lordship's pardon,' murmured Counsel, 'but I have just finished arguing a case before Mr. Justice Field.'

❧   ❧   ❧

A County Court Judge, Mr. Dasent, was also afflicted but stubbornly declined to wear an aid. He was 'hearing' an action over an alleged debt and both parties appeared in person. Unfortunately, neither suspected His Honour's disability.

One of the witnesses, a very pretty girl, was being somewhat savaged in cross-examination.

'You say you are housekeeper to the plaintiff?' asked the defendant. 'Do your functions end there?'

'Yes, yes,' stammered the girl, blushing. 'I don't know what you mean.'

The defendant smiled acidly. 'When we last met, did we not have a conference and discussion about adultery?'

His Honour leaned forward. 'Usury? Usury has nothing at all to do with this case,' he said sharply.

'I said *adultery*.'

'I hear you,' snapped the Judge. 'May I remind you that usury laws have been abolished here these many years.'

'I said adultery,' roared the defendant. 'A-D-U-L-T-E-R-Y.'

'Well, suppose you *have* been committing adultery,' said the Judge severely. 'Nothing whatever to do with this case. I find for the plaintiff—with costs.'

❧   ❧   ❧

Another very deaf Judge in Tipperary would not allow his affliction to interfere in any way with the execution of his duties. He ignored all hints that he might retire or adopt a trumpet and he constantly blamed the acoustics.

As he left the Court one evening after a long case his Clerk ushered him into his room and asked politely if the dispute just decided had been of interest to his lordship.

'Oh, yes, indeed,' piped the old chap. 'I think it was to do with a choral society. Something about the singers disputing over an instrument. *Most* interesting.'

Sad to say, his lordship was in error. The case simply concerned the price of a Singer sewing machine.

♉   ♉   ♉

A certain crotchety Judge could never have been suspected of having any romance left in those hardened old arteries. Perhaps there was a touch of spring in the air that morning when a youth of nineteen was brought before him on a charge of abducting a girl of fifteen.

Counsel for the Crown thundered fire and brimstone and demanded the maximum penalty of two years in gaol. But the Judge had been watching the accused and also the tearful girl over the crescent rims of his spectacles.

Clearing his throat he tried to look severe after the inevitable verdict of 'Guilty'. But those wise, rheumy eyes had not failed to observe that this boy and girl seemed very much in love.

He placed the accused on probation and waggled a long

arthritic finger at him. 'I sentence you both to marriage,' he said in a voice that, for once, had lost all its firmness.

⚏   ⚏   ⚏

Lord Goddard could be severe and forthright but the Press was somewhat inclined to overplay this side. His friends and colleagues saw a different aspect of his character.

He was a superb after-dinner speaker, and his best party piece was to sing or deliver monologues like *Albert and the Lion* in a mock North Country accent.

At a dinner given by the Royal Institute of Chemistry, the Lord Chief Justice read out a question from a recent examination paper: 'What is the effect of a gaseous explosion?'

He then gave the answer in song: 'More work for the undertaker.'

'The Chief' was often quite ruthless towards hardened criminals but more than kindly to others who shared our human frailty. At the end of a day's evidence by a witness who did not seem coherent at all times, he said quietly, 'Tomorrow I strongly recommend tea for breakfast.'

He had little patience with pundits astride their high horses. About a wretched woman who appeared in his Court he observed sharply, 'I've seen some of the tests she had before she was certified. I could not have answered some of them myself.'

Later, in the King's Bench Division, a witness said rather smugly, 'I have never told a lie in my life.'

'Then you are a most remarkable man,' sniffed his lordship.

⊞   ⊞   ⊞

Mr. Justice Wills tolerated no nonsense. He once had before him an elderly gentleman who looked like a bishop but was in fact an expert burglar. When arrested he had said at the station, 'I always tell the truth to my doctor, my lawyer and the police.' This remark was read out in evidence.

The Judge, a charming man but lacking a sense of humour, commented: 'It is obvious that this man is deficient in all moral sense.'

Sad to say, his lordship could not understand why his remark aroused so much laughter in Court.

⊞   ⊞   ⊞

Mr. Justice Channell had two well-marked peculiarities; he spoke with a drawl which maddened Counsel and tortured unfortunate prisoners hanging on to every word of the summing-up and sentence. And, in moments of extreme irritation, he would kick the panel of the bench in front of him.

At the Derby Assizes a man was charged with obtaining food by false pretences. It was an open and shut case and the defence had been weak.

'Do you really need to retire?' his lordship asked the jury.

The jury consulted and decided to stay where they were.

After a minute or two's hurried whispering among themselves, they found the accused 'Not Guilty'.

Channell took a hearty kick at the battered panel and finally mastered his temper. He turned to the jury-box.

'Don't think I'm *quarrelling* with your verdict, gentlemen,' he drawled, 'but it may interest you to know that the man whom you have just acquitted has been convicted before of precisely similar offences upon thirty separate occasions.'

His lordship's tendency to mumble often proved a sore trial to the Bar. After one of his muffled *obiter dicta*, Counsel cupped his ear and asked, 'What was that?'

His learned friend murmured sympathetically, 'Afraid that has been lost in the chops of the Channell.'

ꔷ   ꔷ   ꔷ

Lord Russell of Killowen nodded when the accused asked permission to put a question.

'What is the maximum punishment for bigamy, my lord?'

'Two mothers-in-law,' answered the Judge without hesitation.

ꔷ   ꔷ   ꔷ

Lord Chief Justice O'Brien, familiarly known as 'Pether', had an eye for the ladies. In one case which was going rather badly for the defence, Counsel decided to play his last desperate card and put a girl in the witness-box. Her evidence was not very weighty or relevant but there could be no doubt that she was the prettiest colleen ever to turn a jury's head.

'Pether' certainly thought so and began to warm the defence with his repeated smiles at the witness. Suddenly catching a grin on the face of the cunning barrister, he collected himself.

'This will not do,' he warned Counsel. 'There may have been occasions in the distant past when testimony of this kind might have affected me, but not today. Mr. Kelly, I am now an extinct volcano.'

'I don't know, my lord,' said Kelly graciously. 'There might still be a few rumbles in the old crater yet.'

៣　　៣　　៣

Lawyers, like doctors, have a notorious weakness for talking shop but a certain Lord Justice of Appeal was somewhat embarrassed when a fellow-member of his club, a Jewish K.C., mentioned his disappointment at not having been elevated to the Bench. What hurt most apparently was that the Lord Chancellor had Jewish blood in his veins and might have proved more sympathetic.

'But, my dear fellow,' said the Judge, 'what would you expect from a Jew but a passover?'

៣　　៣　　៣

Women on juries are, of course, a commonplace today but it was not until 1911 that the first mixed jury sat in the Divorce Court. The occasion was marked by some natural confusion, and Counsel for the petitioner soon became bogged.

'Gentlemen—I mean members—you of the jury, six men and six ladies—no, women.' He wiped his brow. 'Let's call you women.'

Not long afterwards the new Judge, Horridge, found himself caught up in the same tangle.

'The word *woman* is scarcely used in this Court now,' he mentioned sadly. 'There are lady clerks, lady assistants, lady charwomen, lady scavengers and lady everything else. I am beginning to wonder whether ladies *are* women.'

      ♉   ♉   ♉

One Judge showed that, jury or no jury, justice was not infallible. Counsel had protested vehemently at not being allowed to call certain witnesses.

'My lord,' he pleaded, 'it surely won't hurt for the evidence to be given! There's no jury to be prejudiced.'

'No, there isn't,' agreed his lordship, 'but there's *me*.'

      ♉   ♉   ♉

A story that has gone the rounds, with many permutations and combinations, concerns three Benchers of the Inner Temple who had dined expansively in that lovely Hall before it was destroyed by Hitler's incendiary bombs.

As they walked out into the silvery moonlight, arm in arm, one of them observed with deep feeling:

'Ah, this would be the perfect night on which to end one's days.'

Upon which they fell to discussing how they would like to die if given the choice.

The youngest, a mere eighty, said he would wish to make a century at Lord's and then fall dead at the wicket, after having scored the winning hit.

The next, five years older, and a famed member of the Pegasus Club in his youth, sighed wistfully and thought that, for him, earth's bliss could end dramatically after he had completed the Grand National course, the first to pass the winning post.

The senior member of the trio, still spry at ninety, snorted his disapproval.

'I don't want to die,' he said firmly, 'but I still hope that, when the time comes, I shall be shot dead by a jealous husband.'

♙   ♙   ♙

Some of Her Majesty's Judges and one or two senior members of the Bar had decided to relax from the strain and dignity of their labours by chartering a steamer to take them to Ramsgate for the day.

Out at sea the boat began tossing about and one of the 'silks' started to crumple. He was leaning wretchedly over the side when a kindly Judge tapped him on the arm and asked sympathetically, 'Can I do anything for you?'

'Yes, indeed,' groaned the stricken one. 'I wish your lordship would overrule this motion.'

PART TWO

The Bar

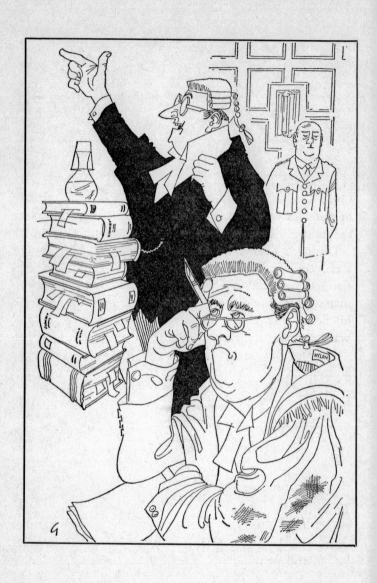

The Bar

ONLY a rash or very adroit witness would risk an exchange of rudeness with learned Counsel. It can boomerang with the most painful results for the man in the box.

During a long and most involved arbitration between a railway company and a local authority, Montague Lush (later a High Court Judge) was confronted by a fat gentleman who claimed to be a rating expert. Fussily, he examined his florid gold watch every few minutes and, obviously, was becoming impatient of the probing questions.

Prodded on several weak points, the witness thought he might score one for himself.

'Remember, Mr. Lush, we are not at the Old Bailey,' he said tartly.

'I don't know why not,' murmured Counsel.

罒   罒   罒

Edward Abinger, who fought so hard for Steinie Morrison's life, was appearing for the defence in another murder trial.

'Will you tell me,' he asked the accused, 'where you were on the night of the murder?'

'Nowheres,' was the unhelpful reply.

'Your reticence places us in a very awkward position,' said his Counsel.

'It is very kind of you gentlemen, but I ain't going to tell any b—— lies, not for nobody!'

◫   ◫   ◫

Abinger appeared in another case before Mr. Justice Hawkins who, as usual, was riding roughshod.

Finally, Counsel was moved to protest: 'Your lordship is trying this question of fact as if a judge and jury were trying it, but without the same power as a jury.'

'Will you kindly tell me what powers a jury have which *I* do not possess?' asked Hawkins icily.

'Why, your lordship can't disagree!' said Abinger with a soothing smile.

◫   ◫   ◫

A woman witness, fashionably dressed and very sure of herself, was proving hard to shake under cross-examination. Counsel had asked her how old she was. She hesitated, blushed very prettily and fluttered appealing eyelashes at the jury.

Then she turned to his lordship and asked permission to write the answer down.

The Judge agreed gallantly.

Without troubling to remove her elegant gloves, which made writing rather difficult, she began very slowly to note the information on a pad.

'Come, come, Lady ——' protested Counsel, 'surely it can't run to three figures!'

* * *

During a petition for divorce on the grounds of cruelty, the wife had stated that the respondent threw a heavy book at her and cut open her head. He was sharply cross-examined about the alleged incident.

'When did this occur?'

'All I can say is that we had a few words,' replied the husband, thinking deeply. 'I was turning over the leaves of a book, when it flew out of my hand.'

'From a circulating library, I suppose?' suggested Counsel.

* * *

A somewhat precious young man, whose only means of support seemed to be a pair of very fancy scarlet braces, made a somewhat unfortunate reply to the opening question in cross-examination.

'What do you do for a living?' he was asked bluntly.

'I live with my aunts.'

* * *

A young lady had reacted very well indeed to a searching cross-examination. As she stepped down from the box, her Counsel, Sir Ellis Hume-Williams, said warmly, 'Please let me congratulate you on the admirable way you gave your evidence.'

'Oh, thank you,' she said with great composure. 'But, you see, I'm a schoolteacher and so quite used to dealing with the questions of children.'

'Thank you,' laughed Counsel. 'I will make sure to mention the fact to my learned friend, the gentleman who cross-examined you.'

Sir Ellis, addressing a jury in a divorce action:

'If ladies should ever lose their habit of keeping diaries, it would destroy one of the few remaining safeguards for the purity of English domestic life.'

F. E. Smith, later Earl of Birkenhead and Lord Chancellor, was a fearless man both inside and outside the Courts. He was always so bursting with vitality that Winston Churchill once said of him that 'he burned all his candles at both ends'.

He was no respecter of Judges with whom he often collided, usually at their expense.

In one case he appeared for a tramway company. The plaintiff was a youth who had been run over by a tram.

It was strenuously claimed that he might suffer blindness as a result of the accident.

Judge Willis, very sentimental by nature, kept saying, 'Poor boy, poor boy! Blind! Put him on a chair so that the jury can see him.'

F.E. was becoming impatient at all this tearful prejudice from the Bench.

'Perhaps your honour would like to have the boy passed round the jury-box?' he growled.

'You are extremely offensive, young man,' said the Judge.

'As a matter of fact, we both are,' was the reply. 'The only difference is that I am trying to be and you can't help it.'

That was certainly not the Judge's best day. Later, he again made the mistake of rebuking the barrister.

'What do you suppose I am on the Bench for, Mr. Smith?'

Counsel smiled very sweetly. 'It is not for me to fathom the inscrutable ways of Providence.'

　　　　　　📖　　　📖　　　📖

In another action for compensation, F.E. employed a manœuvre which is often cited as a classic of legal strategy. This time he represented a bus company sued by the parents of a boy whose left arm was allegedly so damaged that he could only raise it to shoulder level.

In the witness-box he made a pathetic figure, apparently suffering the torments of hell as he sat painfully facing Counsel.

With the jury obviously sympathetic and themselves seasoned bus passengers, F.E. knew instinctively that aggression would not be tactful. Silkily sympathetic and gentle, he proceeded to cross-examine the boy as follows:

'Please lift your left arm as best you can.'

Very gingerly indeed, the witness raised the injured limb up to his shoulder.

'Thank you,' murmured Counsel in a bedside tone. 'And now please will you show us how high you could lift it before the accident?'

Obligingly, the boy shot his arm high up into the air!

📖   📖   📖

Smith's lightning sarcasm had a perfect target in a certain peeress who was claiming under a disputed will. He was cross-examining the lady about an incident when a man friend had apparently tried to make love to her.

'Do you mean to say that he went down on his knees and began to pour out his love?' he asked incredulously.

'I do.'

'Was he stoutish then?'

'The same as he is now.'

F.E. restrained himself from openly winking at the jury. 'When you went to the door, he followed you on his knees, like a man who had had his legs cut off?'

To the amazement of all in Court, the lady promptly went down on hands and knees in the box and demonstrated the passionate manœuvres of her suitor.

F.E. could not resist a parting shot. Keeping a straight face, he asked solemnly, 'Did you walk to the door faster than he waddled or did he waddle faster than you walked?'

He was always at his best if an incautious Judge chose to become testy or unfair. When Counsel rose to make his opening speech, Mr. Justice Ridley so far forgot himself as to observe, 'Well, Mr. Smith, I have read the pleadings and I do not think much of your case.'

F.E. dropped an eyelid at the jury.

'Indeed, I'm sorry to hear that, m'lud, but your lordship will find that the more you hear it, the more it will grow on you.'

⊞ ⊞ ⊞

On another occasion he was arguing an appeal and went on rather too long in elaborating what seemed the obvious. The Bench became restive but F.E. hammered at his point, apparently blind to the irritation and yawnings of the three Judges. Finally, the patience of the Master of the Rolls began to crack.

'Really, Mr. Smith,' he chided, 'do give this Court credit for some little intelligence.'

Quite unabashed, Counsel said, 'That is the mistake I made in the Court below, my lord.'

⊞ ⊞ ⊞

G. D. 'Khaki' Roberts, a fine athlete and brilliant advocate, looks astonishingly like F. E. Smith and has a similar quick wit. In one case at the Old Bailey he was defending two Flying Squad officers.

In an aside to the jury which F.E. would have appreciated,

he observed: 'Because a man joins the Metropolitan Police Force he does not become an angel.'

He once defended an American sailor on a murder charge. The case was heard at the U.S. Naval Headquarters and the proceedings were a trifle informal and sometimes unexpected.

At one point the President mentioned the case of 'The King versus Beddingfield'.

This was too much for 'Khaki' Roberts who jumped up in protest.

'No, no! The Queen! Queen Victoria! That was in 1879, you know.'

◫   ◫   ◫

Patience is a virtue not always possessed by the Bench. Indigestion and other everyday ills are often hidden under the scarlet and ermine.

Tom Jones, a 'silk' on the Northern Circuit, was inclined to be long-winded and leisurely in handling a case involving detail. The Judge was nodding and the jury in a glazed state of coma during one apparently endless speech.

'Mr. Jones, time is passing,' said his lordship wearily.

'Let it pass.'

Several aeons later, the Judge tried again.

'Mr. Jones, there are other cases in the List.'

Counsel bowed stiffly. 'I agree, my lord, there are: but not one save this in which my client takes the slightest interest.'

◫   ◫   ◫

Jones proved not long afterwards that his otherwise sterling qualities did not include a capacity to turn the other cheek.

At Manchester he had had a most heated argument with Mr. Justice Blackburn and left the Court breathing fire from both nostrils.

The following Sunday he was walking round the Botanical Gardens with some friends when the Judge saw them and hurried over, obviously determined to be conciliatory.

Jones turned his back with the cutting remark, 'We are bound to respect Her Majesty's Judges, but we are not bound to speak to them.'

◫   ◫   ◫

The very young advocate, eager to impress the Court (and valuable solicitors), often resorts to eloquence. One tyro was finding the technicalities difficult and sought refuge in more and more words.

The Judge thought fit to net this insect.

'The first time I hear an argument, I appreciate it,' he observed grimly. 'The second time it produces an impression upon me. But after the third time, that impression is effaced.'

The young man recovered smartly. 'Is it, my lord? Then I shall repeat it a fourth time in order that I may revive the first impression.'

◫   ◫   ◫

Not quite so resourceful was a beginner at the Bar who

was terribly nervous in pleading his very first case before
Lord Ellenborough. Fiddling with his gown and plain-
lensed spectacles and adjusting a snowy-white wig, he got
up to deliver his opening address.

'M'lud, in this case my unfortunate client . . .' He swal-
lowed his Adam's apple and began again. 'My unfortunate
client . . .'

'Go on,' the Judge said encouragingly, 'So far the Court
is with you.'

♙   ♙   ♙

As a very young and inexperienced barrister, Frank Lockwood (later Solicitor-General) had the misfortune to appear
before a Judge apparently not quite recovered from jaundice.

'And what are *you* here for?' demanded his lordship
brusquely.

'Just three and one, my lord,' said Lockwood, referring
to the guineas marked on his brief.

♙   ♙   ♙

Lockwood was not only a great wit but an accomplished
quick-sketch artist who amused himself by making drawings
in Court of the witnesses and Judges with whom he was a
great favourite.

One of them invited him to come to his room at the end
of a trial in which the barrister had forced an acquittal after
successfully pleading an alibi.

His lordship congratulated him warmly but Lockwood

brushed this aside modestly and said in his elegant way that it had been a very simple case, really.

'You see, my lord, my client had three alibis. First, that he was at a service in church saying his prayers. Second, that he was with his bookmaker, laying a bet. And third, that he was at the undertaker's buying a coffin for his mother-in-law.'

Lockwood smiled up from the pad on which he was doodling, as usual.

'I told my client that you would like number three best, because you had a mother-in-law. And, so far as I knew, you never said your prayers or laid a bet. So, on my advice, he held on to his mother-in-law's coffin.'

　　　　📖　📖　📖

He was once cross-examining a man who claimed that he had received a blow on the head which had caused him great physical and mental distress.

'Were you really sick or did you only feel sick?' demanded Counsel.

'Well, it's the same thing, isn't it?' shrugged the witness.

'Oh, no,' said Lockwood quickly. 'M'learned friend is sick with me, very sick, but I don't expect that he will throw up his brief.'

　　　　📖　📖　📖

Incredibly enough, Lockwood appeared in a breach of promise action brought by a Miss Week against a Mr. Day.

The parties were, meanwhile, reconciled and announced their intention to marry.

This happy sequel gave Lockwood the inspiration for a little verse which he scribbled on his brief and passed up for the Judge's approval:

'One Day the more, one Week the less,
But we must not complain.
There'll soon be little Days enough
To make a Week again.'

Less diplomatic in his dealings with the Bench was Sir Edward Marshall Hall whose capacity to make judicial enemies almost ruined his practice at one time. His reckless courage once brought him head-on with Mr. Justice Hawkins, a notorious bully who often treated Counsel like inferior servants. His special delight was to keep them hanging about the Court at his whim.

On this occasion, Marshall Hall politely demanded bail for his client, adding, 'the police raise no objection.'

'I don't care a farthing for the police,' roared Hawkins. 'They are not superior to myself at present.'

'Not even, I believe, in their own estimation,' drawled Counsel.

Among Hawkins's other vices was his excessive care of money. During his early days at the Bar he earned a vast income which was far in excess of his expenditure. Stories of his parsimony began to accumulate and one of them deserves, perhaps, to be preserved.

One of his learned friends, married and burdened by a large young family, found himself sitting in Court beside Hawkins, then still a bachelor.

'Tell me, Hawkins,' he asked earnestly, 'why do you take so much care of your money? It can't be of much use to you in this world, and you can't take it with you to the next. Even if you could, it would only *melt*.'

♕   ♕   ♕

During his fighting days at the Bar, Hawkins was famous for his adroitness in dealing with rude Judges of the type he would himself one day become.

He was doing his best in a losing case when the Judge decided to interrupt.

'When you can prove that two blacks make a white, I'll listen to your argument.'

'I can do that, my lord,' said Hawkins evenly. 'I have known a black cock and a black hen produce a white egg.'

♕   ♕   ♕

Hawkins was not the only enemy of Marshall Hall's. During a murder trial when, as usual, he appeared for the defence, he turned passionately to the Judge.

'I implore your lordship to note that this witness has not identified these men.'

'You have said that before,' commented Mr. Justice Grantham with unnecessary sharpness. 'I have not forgotten it.'

'I thought your lordship did not *appreciate* it,' said Counsel acidly.

꒰ꕥ꒱ ꒰ꕥ꒱ ꒰ꕥ꒱

Although not a brilliant lawyer, and with too much of the old Lyceum greasepaint in his make-up, Marshall Hall could think very quickly on his feet.

'Do you ever tell the truth?' he grunted at a witness.

'I try to.'

'Do you ever succeed?' murmured Counsel.

꒰ꕥ꒱ ꒰ꕥ꒱ ꒰ꕥ꒱

Marshall Hall was an authority on precious stones and loved to impress juries with his expertise on a variety of special subjects, including firearms and diamonds.

Sometimes, however, over-confidence led to his undoing. He appeared for a firm of jewellers sued by a peeress who claimed that they had damaged a valuable pearl necklace by over-heating when she had sent it to them for cleaning.

He argued long and learnedly and the jury, as always, hung upon his every word. They watched him in fascination as he stopped now and then to use an inhalant or swallow a pill from the array of drugs and medicines without which he rarely entered Court.

While taking a dose of medicine he failed to notice that

a Hatton Garden merchant was whispering something into the ear of opposing Counsel to whom he handed two pearls. 'Ask Marshall which of the two was burnt,' he suggested, 'and how much it has lost in value as a result.'

Unconscious of a trap, Marshall Hall took the two pearls with some disdain. Always the great showman, he screwed his famous jeweller's glass into his eye and examined them with all the loving care of a suspicious pawnbroker. He then proceeded to make certain other tests with a tremendous flourish, watched by the jury, now in a state of advanced hypnosis.

Finally, he held up one of the pearls and stated with great deliberation that the damage by fire could be confidently estimated at about £500.

'They're duds, as a matter of fact,' said the man from Hatton Garden in a stage whisper. 'You can have 'em both for a bob!'

Counsel stumped out of Court in a rage with the fickle jury's laughter ringing in his ears.

෴   ෴   ෴

Marshall Hall was once asked what was the most unexpected answer he ever received during his many years as a cross-examiner. He replied, without hesitation, that it was during a case when a witness had mentioned that the plaintiff was absent-minded.

'And, pray, do tell the Court how you would define absent-mindedness,' invited Counsel.

'Well,' said the witness slowly, 'I should say that a man

who thought he'd left his watch at home and took it out of his pocket to see if he had time to go home and get it— I should say that chap was a bit absent-minded.'

♛   ♛   ♛

That great lawyer, Charles Russell, who was a solicitor before he went to the Bar and later graced the Bench as Lord Russell of Killowen, was almost as good a judge of human beings as he was of horseflesh. A lesser man would have taken much displeasure from the Judges for his rudeness but Russell had an innocent air and very easy manners. Nobody escaped more lightly in his 'brushes' with the Bench.

He was in the middle of a closely reasoned address when the Judge suddenly snapped out, 'What is your authority for that statement?'

Russell smiled gently and turned to an usher.

'Bring his lordship a book on elementary law,' he said. The roar of laughter only stopped when his pink-faced lordship ordered the Court to be cleared. He didn't interrupt again.

♛   ♛   ♛

But even Russell went too far with his impertinence during a case before Mr. Justice Denman who became so incensed that he could not trust himself to go on. Instead, he adjourned and announced darkly that he would decide on the appropriate action by morning.

There was a crowded Court when the Judge stalked in next day, very stern of face and clearly prepared to issue a harsh rebuke, if not worse.

'Mr. Russell,' he said very solemnly, 'since the Court adjourned last evening I have had the advantage of considering with my brother Judges the painful incident . . .'

'My lord,' Counsel interposed with a graceful little bow, 'I beg you will not say a word more upon the subject, for I can honestly assure you that I have entirely and forever dismissed it from my mind.'

After a second or two, the Judge had recovered enough to join in the laughter.

⊠   ⊠   ⊠

The late Mr. Justice Kekewich had many estimable qualities which did not include a very profound knowledge of the Law. He was so often overruled in the upper Courts that Counsel rather unkindly nicknamed him, 'Necessity'.

One advocate turned these judicial shortcomings to his own advantage in opening his case before the Court of Appeal.

'My lords,' he began cheerfully, 'this is an appeal from the judgment of Mr. Justice Kekewich but I hasten to add that this is not my only ground of appeal.'

⊠   ⊠   ⊠

Another Judge was also somewhat weak in his Law and this led to some breezes with the Bar. A learned but irascible

Attorney-General, appearing before him, behaved in a fashion that would not be tolerated today. His lordship, becoming impatient at one juncture, shouted:

'I ruled that . . .'

'*You* ruled!' sneered the Law Officer. 'You were never fit to rule anything but a copy-book.'

♔   ♔   ♔

Lawyers often suffer at the hands of friends and acquaintances seeking free advice. One barrister, bustling across the 'Bear Garden' at the Law Courts, was accosted by a man whom he knew slightly.

The layman grasped him familiarly by the sleeve and asked his opinion on a point of Law.

'I generally get paid for what I know,' said Counsel haughtily.

The man took out half-a-crown and pressed it into his palm.

'Then tell me all you know and give me the change,' he invited.

♔   ♔   ♔

Lord Bramwell learned once and for all that it is not always wise to try and expedite legal business, however tempting. He was impatiently trying a prisoner on the South Wales Circuit and the verdict was so obviously to be one of 'Guilty' that he became somewhat testy when defence Counsel asked leave to address the jury in Welsh.

However, he gave formal permission for the sentimental gesture, warning Counsel to keep it short. The barrister did so and, to everyone's surprise, the jury wasted no time in bringing in a verdict of 'Not Guilty'.

Later, still shaken, the Judge asked for a note and translation of what the barrister had said to sway the jury so dramatically. It was very brisk and to the point.

'This case, gentlemen, lies in a nutshell. You see exactly how it stands. The Judge is an Englishman, the prosecuting Counsel is an Englishman. But you are Welsh, and I am Welsh, and the prisoner is Welsh. Need I say any more?'

♙   ♙   ♙

Equally terse was the barrister whose key witness had failed to appear. He apologized to the Court in these terms: 'There are seven reasons, m'lud, why the witness in question is unable to attend, the first being that he is unfortunately dead.'

♙   ♙   ♙

While a jury was out considering the facts, the prisoner became more and more anxious as to his fate. He called his Counsel over and whispered, 'Do you think I shall get an honest verdict?'

'I doubt it,' came the cold reply. 'I happen to know that there are two men on the jury who are opposed to capital punishment.'

♙   ♙   ♙

Another client was also inclined to be fussy. At a hurried conference he complained to Counsel, 'You are writing all this on very rough paper.'

'Never mind,' said the barrister sweetly. 'It has to be filed before it comes to Court.'

꒐   ꒐   ꒐

Counsel was cross-examining a bookmaker who had obviously gone far in his profession. He wore a large diamond ring and had modelled himself sartorially on the late Lord Lonsdale. Only a huge Corona was missing to complete the picture of florid elegance.

'Mr. Jones, I believe?' Counsel began.

'That's me.'

'You *are* a bookmaker?'

'I ham.'

'And a very well-dressed ham, too,' commented the barrister.

꒐   ꒐   ꒐

Sir George Jessel was learned and eloquent but he suffered painful difficulties over pronunciation. A snobbish young junior, fresh from Eton and Christ Church, could not contain his surprise.

'Why, he drops his aitches!' he exclaimed in horror.

His leader rounded sternly on him and snapped, 'I would rather drop my aitches with Jessel in hell than aspirate with you in Heaven.'

101

The late Mr. Danckwerts, K.C., was a gifted advocate but somewhat eccentric and verbose. A burly giant, he often made his own rules of procedure and his manner was so intimidating that even the Judges retreated in haste when 'Danky' became aggressive.

He never hesitated to send out for light refreshments, such as beer, milk or hot cocoa during the proceedings, and drank them with obvious enjoyment while his opponent was trying to address the Court. His thirst for liquids was only equalled by his appetite for words and he could rarely be stopped in full tide.

On one memorable occasion, however, he was quietly but effectively doused before the Court of Appeal.

'Why did you not take up that point with the Judge in the lower Court?' asked Lord Justice Romer.

'He stopped me,' bellowed Danckwerts.

'Now, how in the world did he manage to achieve that?' asked his lordship incredulously.

　　　　　♙　　　♙　　　♙

One young Bar student started off a little uncertainly on the road to fame and fortune. At the 'viva' for his Final Examination he was asked what were the conditions necessary to render a marriage valid in Scotland.

He pondered deeply and dredged the following reply from a slightly muddy pool of knowledge: 'For a marriage to be valid in Scotland it is absolutely necessary that it should be consummated in the presence of two policemen.'

4*

A witness was inclined to be smug, a fact which was not lost upon opposing Counsel who waited his moment. With his hands in his pockets, the witness said righteously:

'Well, there's one thing that there's no denying—I never speak maliciously of any man.'

'No, of course not,' murmured Counsel, 'considering that you never talk of anyone but yourself.'

✠   ✠   ✠

Judicial eminence can literally lead to trouble. A barrister suffered from a shortage of inches and tried to compensate by a sharpish manner. Sometimes, however, his handicap proved too much for him. Once he had the misfortune to appear before a rather short-sighted Judge.

'I cannot see you, Mr. ——,' snapped his lordship. 'Will you kindly stand up?'

'I *am* standing up, my lord.'

'Then I am afraid I must trouble you to stand on your seat.'

'I *am* standing on the seat, my lord.'

The Judge tried to be more practical.

'Then you had better add a few Law Reports and stand on them,' he suggested.

Counsel (angrily): 'My lord, I placed six Law Reports on the seat and am at present standing on them.'

✠   ✠   ✠

Judges craving the incense of 'Laughter in Court' can prepare their quips overnight or even during the proceedings. Counsel rarely enjoy this advantage and their best sallies are usually the product of quick thinking.

When the late Mr. Blake Odgers was a young man at the Bar he had the misfortune to appear before a rather pedantic Judge. In the course of his opening address Counsel stated that the prisoner had been sentenced at the Old Bailey.

'The Old Bailey?' tut-tutted the Judge, appearing to be very shocked.

Odgers made a quick recovery and skated deftly round the cracked ice.

'Ah,' he said blandly, 'doubtless your lordship is aware that I am referring to the Central Criminal Court but, knowing your lordship's insatiable thirst for information, I ventured to add the name of the street in which it is situated.'

      ▥   ▥   ▥

Lord Jeffrey mellowed on the Scottish Bench but as an advocate he had an astringent wit. He was addressing the Court during a case in which an army officer was a witness on the other side.

Time and again, he kept referring disdainfully to the man as 'this soldier'. The witness at last became so angry that he stood up and shouted, 'I am not a soldier, I'm an officer.'

Without turning a hair, Jeffrey went on coolly, 'Well, gentlemen of the jury, this officer who on his own statement is no soldier . . .'

      ▥   ▥   ▥

Edward Carson was perhaps the most lethal cross-examiner of all time. Pointing a long index-finger at some unhappy witness, he could discharge invective or sarcasm with equal force.

A classic story concerns his questioning of a ruby-nosed witness.

'I believe ye're a heavy drinker?' he asked in his delightful brogue.

'That's my business!'

'And have you any other business?' murmured Counsel, sitting down on the perfect exit line.

　　　　　🕮　　　🕮　　　🕮

At the Irish Bar he once defended some young friends from Trinity College, Dublin, who had assaulted a welshing bookmaker. They had been stopped just as they were about to throw him into the sea.

'How did ye know they were going to drown you?' asked Carson.

'Is it how did I know?' echoed the indignant victim. 'I knew right enough! Didn't they howld me by the leg over the say wall?'

'Which leg?' asked Counsel innocently: 'Was it your *black* leg?'

　　　　　🕮　　　🕮　　　🕮

Carson was cross-examining a rather shoddy private detective who had, among things, worked as a pawnbroker's assistant. He had also changed his name several times during a varied and colourful career.

'Why did you change your name to Scott?' asked Counsel.

'I had no reason.'

'And why Captain?' persisted Carson.

The witness explained. 'At the office I was called the Boss, the Captain, the Governor, and eventually I took the title of Captain.'

'I see,' said Counsel equably. 'It meant Captain of the Detective Corps. But why Scott? Was it because it reminded you of Great Scott?'

꒐　　꒐　　꒐

But even Carson once had the tables neatly turned on him during a case about the purchase of cattle at a fair.

'Have you got a receipt for the money?' he demanded briskly.

The Irish witness turned pityingly to the Bench. 'Yer honour, I wonder if that man was ever at a fair, and did he ever sell cattle?'

꒐　　꒐　　꒐

In another case, the Judge pointed out that there appeared to be a remarkable discrepancy between the evidence of a carpenter and that of a publican.

'That is so,' Carson agreed mildly. 'Yet another case of difference between Bench and Bar.'

One Irish Judge, Mr. Justice Lawson, was immune to blarney but nevertheless thoroughly enjoyed listening to the many practitioners of that native art. Summing up in a case of pig-stealing, after a long procession of priests, friends and well-wishers had attested to the prisoner's good character, he said genially:

'Gentlemen of the jury, I think the only conclusion you can arrive at is this: the pig was stolen by the prisoner who is the most amiable man in the country.'

♟   ♟   ♟

In Limerick, at the end of a case in which the jury had proved rather more friendly than the facts warranted, the Judge addressed the defendant: 'You go from this Court without a stain on your character, except that you were acquitted by an Irish jury.'

♟   ♟   ♟

A barrister was defending a simple Irish farmer when the pedantic Judge interrupted to ask, 'Has not your client heard of the maxim, *sic utere tuo alienum non laudas*?'

Counsel replied earnestly, 'Not a day passes on which he does not hear it, m'lud. It is the sole topic of conversation where he lives on top of Mushera mountain.'

♟   ♟   ♟

When smuggling was rife off the coasts of Cork, the Customs officers found themselves almost powerless, so cunning were the methods of the smugglers and so unhelpful the local population. At last, some of the fishermen were hauled in for larceny and receiving. One of them admitted the offence but stated that he was not aware that he was doing wrong.

'I understand the prisoner has pleaded guilty,' said prosecuting Counsel.

'He has not,' corrected the Judge. 'He said he did not have the *animus furandi*.'

'Indeed, me lord, I did not,' agreed the accused with some heat. 'Only an old lifeboat, a couple of oars and a small keg.'

☐   ☐   ☐

That great Irish advocate, H. D. Grady, had a trick of winking his right eye at the jury when he wished to impress some special point upon them. He did this with great effect when he was cross-examining a foreign sailor at Cork Assizes.

'You're a Swede, I believe.'

'No, I am a Dane.'

Grady closed his famous eye for the benefit of the jury. 'Gentlemen, you hear the equivocating scoundrel!'

☐   ☐   ☐

Carleton, Lord Chief Justice of Ireland, was a most

gloomy figure on the Bench and a very keen sufferer from acute hypochondria. He was always sorry for himself but usually managed to struggle dismally through the day until he could retire to his bed of imaginary pain.

One morning, however, he arrived late in Court and announced dolefully that he could not carry on. The jury would have to be dismissed.

This time it was not his lordship's health that was troubling him. He explained to the Bar, with a sigh and a tear, that poor Lady Carleton had suffered a miscarriage.

Up jumped Mr. Curran, the senior barrister present.

'Oh, m'lud,' he said winningly, 'I am sure we are quite satisfied that your lordship has done right in deciding there is no *issue* to try today.'

　　　 ▥　　▥　　▥

One Irish advocate, determined to secure a verdict, came into Court more than fully armed. It was an action for goods sold and delivered but unpaid for. The plaintiff argued his case in person and appeared to be in complete mastery of the facts. Counsel for the defendant seemed, however, to be unusually confident.

'Your honour, these were probably goods supplied to the wife without authority,' he suggested.

'The defendant has no wife,' put in the plaintiff.

'Well, your honour, I rely on the Statute of Limitations.'

'The goods were supplied this year,' smiled the plaintiff.

'I mean, of course, your honour, the Tippling Act,' amended Counsel, quite unabashed.

'This was all hardware; I don't sell drink.'

'What about the Sale of Goods Act?' floundered the barrister.

'Sure and he walked out with the stuff,' pointed out the plaintiff, scenting victory.

'Well, your honour, I had to suggest every sort of defence because my client has not come in to instruct me properly.'

'Then I'll decree him,' said the Judge firmly.

Counsel shook his head. 'Sure, your honour, ye can't do that, because he's dead. He was buried yesterday.'

        ❦   ❦   ❦

Many of the old Irish Judges and barristers were fond of riding to hounds, and a local Meet would play havoc with the legal List. One keen sportsman dashed into Court to make an application with his black gown thrown hurriedly over his white breeches and other sporty garments.

As he began to address the Court, his coat, which was rather too tight, expanded and revealed all the glory within.

'I cannot hear you, sir,' said the Judge who was no follower of the hunt.

Counsel collected himself at once. 'Your lordship is not suggesting that it is my waistcoat that you cannot hear?' he purred winningly. 'I admit it looks *loud* enough.'

        ❦   ❦   ❦

Tim Healy was celebrated for the sharpness of his wit. In an action over some timber, he represented the defendant and was surprised to see that the expert put up by the other side was little more than a boy. This was meat and drink to Healy who contented himself with a very crisp cross-examination indeed.

'How old are you?' he asked.

'Twenty-one.'

'And how long have you been in the timber business?'

'Two years.'

Healy turned to the Judge with raised bushy eyebrows. 'A regular babe in the wood, my lord,' was his crushing comment.

But he had a rare reverse in another case in Dublin. The witnesses were about to be sworn but nobody could find the Bible. A frantic search began until opposing Counsel noticed that Healy was reading the Book with great concentration. He handed it quickly to the usher and expressed his regret.

His learned friend smiled at the Judge.

'We quite understand, my lord. Mr. Healy was so absorbed that he did not appreciate our loss. He took it for a new publication.'

᠁ ᠁ ᠁

Lord Birkett has rightly been credited with having exhibited the most perfect manners while at the Bar and on the Bench. Although the most successful advocate of his day, he was never guilty of sarcasm or the bullying of witnesses. He used a bedside manner in cross-examination which rarely went beyond gentle irony. Only his closest associates knew how great a strain he endured during some of the dramatic murder trials with which he was so often associated.

After a successful defence in a murder trial, he returned to his Chambers in the Temple, threw his wig on the table and slumped into a chair, exhausted.

'This sort of case takes years off a man's life,' he said wearily to his junior.

'Maybe,' agreed Dingle Foot, 'but they add years to his client's.'

ꑮ ꑮ ꑮ

I recall one case when Norman Birkett appeared for a man who was claiming damages for injuries suffered in a taxi-cab smash.

Counsel cross-examined the driver who, in his own view, had been driving at a snail's pace.

'You skidded slightly?' murmured Counsel. The witness agreed.

'Mounted the pavement?' A nod from the cabby.

'You hit a plate-glass window and smashed it?'

'Right.'

'Knocked over two or three stalls loaded with fruit and vegetables?'

'Correct.'

'Knocked down one policeman and two pedestrians?'

'I'm afraid so,' agreed the witness.

'And finally knocked down a lamp-post?'

'Yes.'

Birkett paused to twiddle his gold pencil, a characteristic gesture, before the final thrust.

'Well,' he said slowly, 'I wonder if you would like to estimate how much more damage you might have done if you had been going fast?'

༄ ༄ ༄

Sir Patrick Hastings, an old friendly adversary, once re-marked after a murder trial:

'If ever it had been my lot to take a lady for a stray week-end and then decided to cut her into small pieces and place her in an unwanted suitcase, I should unhesitatingly have placed my future in Norman's hands.

'He would have satisfied the jury (a) that I wasn't there; (b) that I had not cut up the lady; (c) that if I had, she had thoroughly deserved it.'

༄ ༄ ༄

Sir Patrick himself was the master of the *coup de grâce*. A witness had been examined elaborately on his length of service, and Counsel rose to cross-examine.

'You have been with your firm for sixty-one years?' he asked.

'Settling down well?' murmured Sir Patrick.

༄ ༄ ༄

While new at the Bar and still inclined to be rather aggressive, Hastings was cross-examining a witness who, some months previously, had been a client of his.

'You will not give your answers like that, if you take my advice,' he threatened.

'I will not take your advice,' said the witness firmly. 'I took it once and went to prison for twelve months.'

◫   ◫   ◫

Women witnesses are notoriously difficult to handle, even by their own Counsel. They become chatty or temperamental and dangerously averse to giving a plain 'yes' or 'no'.

Under cross-examination, they can be touchy and sharp of tongue, as Hastings learned when he began to prod a woman about her past life. She retaliated by mentioning a quite innocent party and discrediting him.

Hastings rebuked her severely. 'I hope you are sorry to have made those statements.'

She blinked her eyelashes. 'Indeed, I am,' she said sweetly. 'Just as sorry as *you* were when you asked me those questions about my past life.'

◫   ◫   ◫

That great advocate, William Ballantine, had an amusing if unexpected experience during his early days at the Bar. Still a fledgling with a very white wig and a very blue bag, he was being continually prodded by his instructing solicitor.

He was cross-examining a witness when the solicitor

suggested a question. Ballantine put it and the witness replied.

'That's a lie,' snapped the solicitor.

More questions were fed by the client with the same result. 'Lies—lies. He's a liar, he always was a liar, and always will be a liar.'

Counsel was becoming rather nettled.

'You seem to know all about him,' he commented sarcastically.

'Of course I do,' said the solicitor. 'He's my son.'

⊞   ⊞   ⊞

At the Brewster Sessions, Counsel noticed that his junior kept interrupting his application for the renewal of a licence by smiling openly at one of the women magistrates.

'Don't do that,' growled the leader. 'It isn't done! If we need to do that sort of thing, please leave it to me. I think it was perfectly disgraceful the way you ogled that member of the Bench. From experience, I can assure you it will do us no good.'

'Which one do you mean?' asked the junior.

'Why, that good-looking and well-dressed woman on the Chairman's left.'

'Oh,' said the young man. 'That's my mother.'

⊞   ⊞   ⊞

A certain Judge made the mistake of trying to heckle the very adroit and experienced Serjeant Ballantine.

'Really, this is a long way from the point,' he said testily.

'I am well aware of that, my lord,' replied the urbane Q.C. 'But if I were to begin any nearer, the witness would discover my object.'

⊞   ⊞   ⊞

Mr. Oswald, a most painstaking advocate, was arguing at length and learnedly on the law of detinue and trover.

'And now, my lord,' he observed. 'I will address myself to the furniture.'

Rather exhausted, the Judge sighed, 'You have been doing that for a long time, Mr. Oswald.'

But the same Counsel had his revenge in another case.

'I may teach you law, Mr. Oswald,' said the Judge, 'but I cannot teach you manners.'

'No, my lord, I know you can't,' said Counsel tartly.

⊞   ⊞   ⊞

At one time, several shady clerks practised illegally as solicitors and used the name of an attorney named Hills who apparently received a percentage for his co-operation. It seemed that Hills was so busy that he was practising all over the country, and at the same time.

The malpractice was becoming such an open scandal that the Bench thought it time to take some action. During one case the Judge suddenly interrupted to say, '*What* is Mr. Hills? *Where* is Mr. Hills? *Who* is Mr. Hills?'

To his lordship's great surprise, a seedy-looking individual,

117

apparently suffering from chronic catarrh, shuffled forward and said, 'I am Mr. Hills.'

Counsel for the other side at once jumped to his feet and said excitedly, 'My lord, my lord, let him be marked *as an exhibit.*'

☐   ☐   ☐

Rufus Isaacs, later Lord Chief Justice, had a suave but deadly quality as a cross-examiner. His quiet, almost diffident manner often proved the undoing of witnesses who mistook it for weakness.

He was gently pin-pricking a man charged with fraud and the wholesale manipulation of balance sheets.

'Why were so many transactions left out of the minutes at meetings over which you presided?' asked Counsel in his silky voice.

'Would you like me to be chairman and secretary and everything?' roared the accused.

'No, I think you were enough,' commented Rufus Isaacs.

☐   ☐   ☐

He again showed this deadly irony in a 'Society' divorce action which involved a hard-fought battle for the custody of the child. One of the odd features of this infernal triangle was that the co-respondent occupied a room next to the wife's, while her husband had a room at the other end of the house.

Rufus Isaacs questioned the husband about this strange arrangement.

'Was not the room he (the co-respondent) occupied the one you, as the lady's husband, should have occupied instead of being given over to a stranger?'

'I did not consider him a stranger,' snapped the witness.

'I agree,' said Isaacs very quietly.

⊞　　⊞　　⊞

A cruel joke was played by Henry Hawkins while he was at the Bar. At that time the Criminal Courts had a character named Best who was nicknamed 'Second-Best' because he often defended for smaller cut-price fees which his learned friends had turned down. He was a melancholy looking fellow, always rather down-at-heel, and the butt of his colleagues.

He was about to address a jury on behalf of his client when the usher handed him a large envelope sealed with black wax and bound with black ribbon. Poor Best opened it quickly. It contained a black tie and a pair of black kid gloves. And Hawkins had enclosed a little note which read: 'I thought you might care to have these when you go into mourning for your client.'

⊞　　⊞　　⊞

In the old days, proceedings at Bow Street were sometimes enlivened by 'noises off' from the adjacent market. While

Counsel was speaking at some length, a coster's donkey was heard to bray very loudly.

Counsel on the other side could not resist his opportunity. 'My learned friend is always received with musical honours,' he commented unkindly.

♬   ♬   ♬

Irony can backfire, as Charles Bowen discovered to his cost on a celebrated occasion. While on circuit, he delivered his final address for the Crown in a foolproof case of housebreaking.

'If you believe, gentlemen,' he told the jury majestically, 'that the prisoner considered the housetops the proper place for an evening stroll, and by pure accident he happened to have about him the necessary tools of a housebreaker with no dishonest intention of employing them, you will, of course, acquit him.'

Listening intently, the jury did exactly that!

♬   ♬   ♬

A man sought to restrain the local authority from opening a smallpox centre near his property because of the danger of infection. He enlisted the aid of a doctor who proved anything but an asset in the box.

Counsel asked smoothly, 'I understand you to say that if with one patient there would be a risk of infection at, say, ten yards, with two at twenty yards, and so on, it follows

that if there were a thousand patients there would be risk of infection several miles away.'

'Exactly, that is my meaning,' was the incredible reply, and even the emotionless Mr. Justice Pearson was finding it hard to look impassive.

But worse was to come. Counsel went on genially, 'Well, it has nothing to do with this case, but for the satisfaction of his lordship and myself, will you tell me some place in London where we should be comparatively free from infection?'

The unfortunate doctor thought deeply and said, 'The middle of Hyde Park.'

♊   ♊   ♊

Counsel was cross-examining a long-haired seedy individual.
  'What are you?'
  'A poet.'
  'A poet! Do you make a living by it?'
  'Yes, I keep the wolf from the door.'
  'What, by reading your poems to him?'

♊   ♊   ♊

Ridicule is the sharpest weapon in Counsel's armoury but it must be fired accurately and, above all, be shafted with surprise.

In an action over the loss of a ship which the underwriters claimed had been scuttled, the chief witness was the captain of the vessel. He fared badly under questioning and was caught napping in one mis-statement after another.

Finally, out of the blue and delivered with great innocence, came the knockout blow.

'On what ship did you come over from America to give evidence?' asked Sir William Jowitt, who of course knew perfectly well.

'*The George Washington*, sir,' answered the unsuspecting skipper. He alone did not join in the roar of laughter that rocked the Court.

✻ ✻ ✻

Balfour Browne, a leading figure at the Parliamentary Bar, had a sharp tongue in a very shrewd head. In a certain difficult case he was confronted by a bumptious man who entered the box with a long pencil stuck behind his ear.

Counsel lost no time in unbalancing this witness. 'Would you remove that pencil?' he demanded firmly. 'I cannot examine a moulting porcupine.'

In an important appeal, he was constantly twitted by a Lord Justice who rudely accused him of contradicting himself.

'My lord,' said B.B., 'one of us is labouring under a mental aberration, and it is not I.'

✻ ✻ ✻

A certain advocate was noted for his unorthodox and often quite unethical tactics. On one occasion he was perhaps justified when a Circuit Judge tried to use excessive influence on the jury.

His lordship was inclined to be suspicious of country juries who are so often subject to prejudice and local patriotism. Anxious to insure against this, the Judge summed up as follows: 'You are bound, of course, to convict the prisoner but no one need think that this would expose him to a severe sentence.' All this was delivered in a coaxing tone designed to lull the most suspicious.

Counsel for the defence quickly wrote something down on a slip of paper and managed to have it passed to the jury. On it he had written the terse warning, 'About ten years'.

After a very few moments, the foreman stood up. 'Not Guilty,' he announced in a strong voice.

♨   ♨   ♨

In the old days of rotund eloquence, juries were the target for some remarkable oratory. Counsel were usually convinced that a weak case might be usefully garnished and served up to impress those in Court, particularly solicitors with future briefs.

During a long libel action, Counsel addressed the jury with some feeling:

'Gentlemen, my client is a cheese merchant in the City of London, and the reputation of a cheese merchant in the City of London is like the bloom on a peach—touch it, and it is gone for ever.'

♨   ♨   ♨

A breach of promise suit has always offered poetic scope to advocates for the heartbroken plaintiff.

Counsel once concluded his exposure of a defendant's wickedness by saying, 'And, gentlemen, this serpent in human shape stole the heart of my virgin client while she was returning from Confirmation.'

⌘ ⌘ ⌘

In a landlord and tenant dispute, the Judge was puzzled to hear the tenant described as being 'in the autumn of his life'. He looked far from aged and indeed so virile that His Honour felt bound to ask how old he was, in fact.

'He is fifty-one,' explained Counsel.

Counsel for the other side jumped up at once. 'If my friend is right, m'lud, then I must be frost-bitten and in the hard grip of winter. I'm sixty-five.'

⌘ ⌘ ⌘

Mr. Murphy's pleading always carried great weight. He also tipped the scales at twenty stone.

'Do you move?' asked the Judge during a hearing.

'With difficulty, your lordship,' Murphy confessed sadly.

⌘ ⌘ ⌘

The genial Sir Henry Curtis Bennett was also built on ample lines and often won sympathy by laughing at himself.

'Is there no one on the other side, Sir Henry?' asked a Judge, peering forward.

'Yes, my lord. But my learned friend is obscured by my body. I apologize.'

In another case before a County Bench, one of the magistrates intervened to ask: 'What I want to know is how tubercular cows can be recognized. How is one to tell exactly whether a cow is tubercular or not?'

'So far as I can make out,' suggested Sir Henry blandly, 'a normal cow is built somewhat on my lines, whereas a tubercular cow is built on the lines of my learned friend.'

In an overcrowded Court the ventilation was poor and the day very hot. The Bench had wilted and was becoming a trifle prickly in mood. Curtis turned this, as usual, to advantage.

'I quite agree,' he cooed, 'that it is very hot, but if you will quickly decide in favour of my application, then there will be much more breathing-space in Court.'

Once he wrote a letter to his old friend, Sir Travers Humphreys: 'I am, as you know, the Master for the present year of that ancient City Guild, the Gold and Silver Wyre Drawers. We should be very greatly honoured if you would be our guest at our forthcoming banquet.'

'My dear Henry,' came the sly reply, 'I thank you very much for your invitation. I accept it with alacrity. The prospect of seeing you with gold and silver wire drawers makes it irresistible.'

◪　◪　◪

Curtis was always a great favourite with juries who warmed to his urbane manner. 'You may think my client is a fool,' he said in a closing speech. 'I tell you so myself—he *is* a fool. But you can't convict on that or the Courts would be full.'

Once he was opposed by his son, Derek, to whom he referred genially as 'My young and learned friend whose name I seem to recognize'.

⋈ ⋈ ⋈

A barrister named Prendergast might have gone far but for his slovenly habits and his inevitable custom of keeping the Court waiting. A tall gaunt figure, dressed in rusty black clothes well past darning, he looked more like a scarecrow after a storm than a member of an Honourable and Ancient Inn of Court.

Slowly and inevitably he sank to becoming little more than a mouthpiece for debt-collectors. Magistrates finally grew less tolerant of his appearance and manners.

One scene before a City Bench has never been repeated. 'Mike' Prendergast strolled into Court, late as usual, and the magistrates eyed him with disapproval which he ignored, relapsing into his normal brown study.

When his turn came to address the Bench, he was sharply nudged awake by his long-suffering Clerk.

'Fred,' he roared. 'Where's my brief?'

'I gave it to you at breakfast,' said Fred sharply. 'Feel in your pockets.'

Prendergast began his search and finally unearthed a wad

of buttered toast to which adhered the solicitor's instructions. Quite unperturbed, he glanced over the grubby papers and then made out an excellent case for his client.

॥ ॥ ॥

Two barristers had long been great rivals but the race was clearly being won by Mr. Phillips who was not only very handsome but had the Irishman's gift of repartee. His learned friend, Mr. Adolphus, had lost much of his practice mainly because he so often lost his temper.

During one case Adolphus turned savagely on the opposing Counsel and shouted, 'You remind me of three B's—blarney, bully and bluster.'

'Ah,' said Phillips suavely. 'You never complained of my B's until they began to suck your honey.'

॥ ॥ ॥

A barrister of this period committed the almost perfect crime of unconscious humour during an action in which an insurance company was disputing a doubtful claim.

A long procession of witnesses had been called and the unfortunate Judge was becoming more and more impatient. After a very prosy examination of a medical witness, Counsel studied his brief for a moment or two before continuing.

'And who is your next witness?' demanded his lordship.

'Well, my lord,' replied the barrister, 'having called the doctor, the next in order will be the undertaker.'

When the future Mr. Justice Eve expressed his intention
to take 'silk', one of his seniors wrote back to him:

> 'My dear Eve,
> Whether you wear silk or fig-leaf
> I do not care
> A. Dam.'

PART THREE

The Box

The Box

REPARTEE is to be expected from barristers trained to think quickly and to use their tongues either as crowbars or rapiers. From their superior position on the Bench, Her Majesty's Judges are even more favourably placed to offer wit, and sometimes wisdom, to lesser mortals. And their lordships can usually expect a respectful Press to report remarks which lighten the gloom of the Courts.

Yet, from the time of David and Goliath, if not before, it has been comforting to the human spirit to applaud the triumph of the little man.

Buried under the scarlet and ermine, badgered by pompous 'silks', and often groping in a maze of quibble and technicality, the nervous layman has now and then suddenly thrown his cloth cap in the air and aimed a well-charged catapult at the wigs, full-bottomed and otherwise.

◫　　◫　　◫

A very old lag charged with robbery seemed to be certain of being sentenced to penal servitude as an habitual offender. The prosecution had made it clear that his testimony was unreliable in every way and the Judge summed up dead against him. Besides, he had confessed to his crime.

Somehow, the jury seemed to be touched by the spectacle of this legal juggernaut remorselessly crushing a tiny insect. They brought in a verdict of 'Not Guilty'. Amazed, the Judge asked them to retire again and reconsider their verdict. Back they came with a stolid 'Not Guilty'.

The Judge passed a dazed hand over his chin, and in a croak of disbelief asked the reason, since the man had already confessed.

'There is reason enough, my lord,' said the foreman. 'For we all know him to be one of the greatest liars in the country.'

　　　　　🛝　　🛝　　🛝

Mr. Justice Jelf had summed up most patiently and exhaustively and, after several hours of profound analysis of all the issues involved, he left the matter with confidence in the hands of the jury.

They retired but at the end of half a day's deliberation returned to announce that they had been quite unable to arrive at a verdict.

'What is your difficulty?' inquired his lordship in surprise.

'Only one thing, my lord,' answered the foreman. 'We just want to know what this case is all about.'

　　　　　🛝　　🛝　　🛝

In a murder trial the case centred upon two simple questions.

Was the victim hit? Alternatively, did he die as a result of a fall?

After a very long retirement, the jury filed back. The foreman cleared his throat and said solemnly: 'We find that the deceased died from a blow. If the prisoner administered the blow, it was wilful murder. If it was the doorstep, it was manslaughter.'

※ ※ ※

The sly and knowing juryman asked very confidently to be excused from service because he was deaf in one ear. But the Judge had heard that one before and shook his wise old head.

'Oh, you'll do,' said his lordship reassuringly. 'We only hear one side of the case at a time.'

※ ※ ※

Baron Alderson, on the other hand, took a different view and once released a juryman who admitted he was deaf in one ear.

'Please leave the box before the trial begins. It is necessary that the jury should hear both sides.'

※ ※ ※

One Circuit Judge was incensed that a jury had acquitted the accused of horse-stealing when the evidence against him was quite conclusive. Just as the man was leaving the dock, his lordship said warmly:

'Luckily for you, you have been found Not Guilty by the jury, but you know perfectly well you stole that horse. You may as well tell the truth, as no harm can happen to you now by a confession. You cannot be tried again. Now, tell me, did you not steal that horse?'

The man scratched his ear. 'Well, my lord,' he said pleasantly, 'I always thought I did until I heard my Counsel's speech, but now I begin to think I didn't!'

✦ ✦ ✦

At the Dublin Assizes a man was convicted of bigamy. In passing sentence the Judge expressed horror that any man could be such a double-dyed villain as to delude several innocent women.

'Please, your lordship,' protested the accused, 'I was only trying to get a good one.'

✦ ✦ ✦

At the Durham Assizes two neighbours were haggling over a trivial claim and patently wasting the time of the Court. Finally, the Judge hinted that Counsel might ask his client what she would accept to settle the action. Unfortunately, the lady was very deaf and the barrister's stage whisper echoed through the Court.

'His lordship wants to know what you will take,' he roared after several attempts.

THE BOX

'That's very kind of his lordship,' said the plaintiff with a winning smile. 'If it's no inconvenience, I'll take a light ale.'

☐ ☐ ☐

The prison visitor was dealing with a hardened character without perhaps knowing it.

'What brought you to gaol?' he asked sympathetically.

'Two constables, sir,' said the man.

'Yes, yes, but had intemperance anything to do with it?'

'Yes, sir,' agreed the prisoner respectfully. 'They were both drunk.'

☐ ☐ ☐

A pink-faced young P.C. was giving evidence on his very first Police Court case. It was a charge of burglary and the newcomer had carefully prepared his notes which he read out solemnly.

The magistrate's first question put him quite off gear.

'Who was in the house?' he demanded.

'Please, your worship, I was the only person present in the house except another constable who was outside.'

☐ ☐ ☐

A rather bovine P.C. was being minced in cross-examination by the clever 'silk'.

'What exactly was the prisoner doing?' he demanded.

'He was arguing with the taxi-driver,' said the witness.

'Ah,' sniffed Counsel. 'Do you think that proves he was drunk?'

'No,' agreed the constable with a slow grin. 'But, you see, there wasn't a taxi-driver there.'

✴   ✴   ✴

A passer-by had reported that a woman was drunk.

The magistrate thought it was a borderline case and began to quiz the witness.

'Why are you so absolutely sure that she was the worse for drink?' he probed.

'Well, sir,' replied the witness, 'because she was in the middle of the road trying to pick up the white line.'

✴   ✴   ✴

'How old are you?' the Judge asked of a rather coy witness.

'Thirty.'

'Thirty!' echoed the Judge. 'I have heard you give the same age in this Court for the last three years.'

The lady looked irritated. 'I'm not one of those people who say one thing one day and another the next,' she said tartly.

✴   ✴   ✴

Irish wit is by no means limited to the lawyers. One witness was being jockeyed rather roughly in the box but, for his own good reasons, which perhaps included a vast liquid lunch, he declined to answer any questions.

The Judge fixed him with a baleful eye.

'This is Contempt of Court,' he thundered.

'I know it, my lord,' said the obstinate one, 'but I was endeavouring to conceal it.'

◫　◫　◫

During the same Assize, through which the waters of the Liffey had flowed merrily, a Judge became impatient of certain frank comments on his ancestry which floated down from the public gallery. In a harsh tone he ordered the usher to clear the Court.

That official swayed to his feet and in a more or less firm voice called out, 'All ye blaggards that aren't lawyers, lave the building.'

◫　◫　◫

On an Irish Circuit, a criminal case was called but the indictment was quashed on a technical point.

The Judge was about to call for the next case when a man rushed into Court, looking very hot and flushed.

'Shall I be in time for Flanagan's case?' he asked breathlessly.

'It is over,' said the Judge. 'Why do you wish to know?'

'Faith! I'm witness for the defence. Am I too late then?'

'Oh, no,' said the Judge kindly. 'Anyway, he was acquitted.'

'Begorra, yer honour, he must have had a dale of influence!'

𝕎　　𝕎　　𝕎

Before an Irish Bench a man was charged with stealing a horse. The magistrate eyed him sharply and thought that a little terror might be in order as this was a district in which horses had a habit of disappearing most mysteriously and usually at night.

'Yours is a very serious offence,' he said solemnly. 'Seventy years ago, it was a hanging matter.'

'Exactly,' agreed O'Reilly with some warmth. 'And seventy years from now it mayn't be a crime at all. Why not postpone sentence for a while and see how things work out?'

𝕎　　𝕎　　𝕎

When Patrick, a pugilistic bricklayer, was charged with assault, the Judge shook his head sadly.

'I wouldn't think you would hit a little man like that.'

'Suppose he called *you* an Irish slob?' protested Pat vehemently.

'But I'm not an Irishman,' said the Judge.

'Suppose he called you a Welsh slob?'

'I'm not a Welshman.'

Pat was visibly trying to keep his patience. 'Well, suppose he called you the kind of slob ye are?'

𝕎　　𝕎　　𝕎

THE BOX

In County Cork, a very successful English lawyer was making rather heavy weather of his cross-examination of a witness who skated most expertly over the thin ice that sometimes separates fact from fiction. To make matters worse, the jury seemed to be enjoying the foreigner's discomfiture.

Thoroughly rattled, the Q.C. decided on a frontal assault.

'Do you know the nature of an oath?' he said brusquely.

'I do, indade.'

'Are you not aware that you are commanded by the Holy Book not to bear false witness against your neighbour?'

'I am,' shouted Patrick, red in the face. 'But sure I'm not bearing false witness against him, I'm bearing it *for* him.'

🔲　🔲　🔲

In his relaxed moments, Serjeant Sullivan loved to tell stories of Irishmen who failed to attend for jury-service. One produced a medical certificate which read: 'This is to certify that I attended Timothy Driscoll this day and found him suffering from contusion upon the lower dorsal region, haemorrhage of the post-nasal vessels and acute echymosis of the dexter orbit.'

'Very interesting,' said the Judge. 'Fined two pounds.'

He was more sympathetic to a letter from a woman: 'My husband died ten years ago but the rate collector had drink taken and put back his name in the book.'

🔲　🔲　🔲

A banking house had behaved somewhat carelessly with some of their clients' funds. One of the victims was about to enter the witness-box when he stumbled.

'I hope you are not hurt,' said the kindly Judge.

'Oh no, my lord, I have only lost my balance.'

Just before hearing a trial at the Old Bailey, the Recorder was astonished to observe an additional man in the jury-box. He polished his glasses, counted again and naturally demanded an explanation.

A tall sad-looking man in deepest black stood up in the box.

'My lord,' he said gloomily, 'I am afraid I am the cause of the confusion. I am in the list of jurymen for tomorrow but I have just lost my dear wife.' He took out a huge handkerchief and began to sob into it.

The Recorder, much distressed, kindly expressed his sympathy and agreed to release him from service.

'Thank you, my lord,' said the sad one, 'but I would rather serve today, if you will allow me.' He blew his nose. 'I think the business of the Court will distract my attention and help me for the time being to forget my loss. Perhaps one of the other gentlemen will leave the box now, and will serve for me tomorrow, when I have to attend the funeral.'

The Recorder granted permission.

The law as to criminal insanity is rather complex and the Judge had been at considerable pains to explain the McNaughton Rules for the guidance of the jury. They did not take long to reach a verdict.

The foreman stood up and announced gravely, 'We are all of one mind—insane.'

※　※　※

A man charged with burglary bore on his face the trade-marks of his former occupation, including a broken nose and a tin ear. The Clerk asked him if he would like to challenge any of the jurors.

Slightly punch-drunk, he stared fixedly at the box and said thoughtfully:

'I'm rather out of training, but I don't mind taking on the little chap with glasses in the front row.'

※　※　※

One jovial-looking man who always attended the Old Bailey on his visits to London usually took a glass of wine in the refreshment room. Invariably he raised it with the respectful toast, 'To their lordships, bless 'em. My grateful thanks for past favours and for favours to come.'

On hearing this, one barrister asked another who this man was.

'Oh,' said his friend, 'that's Calcraft, the hangman.'

※　※　※

143

A certain barrister was inclined to drive too fast on his way home from the Courts. On one sad occasion he ran over and killed a particularly ugly dog.

Much distressed, he got out and apologized to the owner of the animal.

'Murderer!' she shrieked, and a crowd began to gather.

Hot under his wing collar, the barrister again expressed his regrets.

'Madam,' he groaned in despair, 'I will replace your dog.'

'You flatter yourself,' she replied icily.

⋈ ⋈ ⋈

A barrister, notorious for his rough tactics, met his Waterloo while cross-examining a recently promoted police officer.

'When were you made Inspector?' he demanded offensively.

'On the same day, sir, that you were made a Q.C.'

⋈ ⋈ ⋈

The supposedly slow-witted country policeman has often been a favourite target in the witness-box. At the Winchester Assizes a German waiter was charged with stealing a bicycle. It was not a serious case and Mr. Justice Bigham, with a heavy List ahead, was anxious to press on. Unhappily every question and answer had to be translated by an interpreter for the benefit of the accused.

The stolid Hampshire constable gave his evidence very deliberately. 'Acting on information received, I went to the

public bar of the —— Hotel where I saw the prisoner. I said to him, "Did you come here on that bicycle?" He said, "Yes, I did." I then said to him, "Does that bicycle belong to you?" He said, "No, it belongs to a friend of mine who has been kind enough to lend it to me for the afternoon." '

'Stop!' ordered the Judge impatiently. 'In what language did you hold this conversation with the prisoner?'

'In English, my lord.'

'What!' thundered his lordship. 'Does he understand English?'

'He did when *I* spoke to him, my lord,' said the constable with a sly smile.

꒐   ꒐   ꒐

Horatio Bottomley, editor, politician and share-pusher, was once told by Marshall Hall that he could have made a brilliant career for himself at the Bar. Before he was finally nailed and sent to penal servitude, he proved more than a match for most of the formidable advocates who cross-examined him.

'Now, Mr. Bottomley,' said Counsel in one of these numerous cases, 'I am going to ask you a very serious question.'

'Ah,' sighed the old scoundrel, 'no doubt to distinguish it from your earlier ones.'

꒐   ꒐   ꒐

Even a long spell in prison could not kill his sardonic sense of humour. He had been out only a few days and was lunching at Romano's when Sir Henry Curtis Bennett came over and said genially, 'How well you're looking.'

Bottomley stared at the K.C.'s ample paunch. 'It looks as if three years wouldn't do you much harm either,' he laughed.

🔲　　🔲　　🔲

After successfully defending a libel action, Bottomley turned to a friend and remarked:

'What a nice old gentleman on the Bench! He let me say what I liked. I think I shall retain him to hear all my future cases.'

🔲　　🔲　　🔲

Sir John Simon was examining a witness with his usual courtesy and thoroughness. But this time he received rather more than he had bargained for.

'So, Mr. Bottomley invited you to luncheon, Mr. Murray,' he said gently. 'Please tell the jury what happened.'

'Well,' said the witness, thinking hard, 'I arrived at the restaurant and an attendant took my hat and coat and I went and washed my hands.'

'Yes, yes,' said Simon patiently, 'but what happened at the actual luncheon?'

'First of all, we had some hare soup and dumplings. Yes, I'm sure there were dumplings. Then we had fried smelts; and then—yes, to be sure—Mr. Bottomley ordered two portions of roast saddle of mutton.'

Simon controlled himself with a great effort. He tried again. 'Yes, yes, Mr. Murray, but . . .'

This was too much for Bottomley who was thoroughly enjoying himself. He jumped to his feet and protested to the Judge in mock anger.

'I really must ask your lordship to stop learned Counsel interrupting his own witness. What about the vegetables? *The vegetables*.'

📖   📖   📖

Nobody could be more urbanely offensive than Horatio Bottomley, as he proved during cross-examination before the Official Receiver.

'You keep racehorses?' asked Counsel.

'No,' said Bottomley.

'But you did keep racehorses?'

'No, never.'

'You have a place in Sussex called The Dicker?'

'Yes.'

'You have stables there—large stables?'

'Yes.'

'You breed horses there—racehorses?'

'Yes.'

'Then why did you tell me that you never kept racehorses?'

Bottomley smiled. 'I gave you a correct answer. I never kept racehorses. They keep me.'

📖   📖   📖

Not all lay advocates have proved as gifted as Bottomley. Many of them run a grave risk in handling their own cases and often let over-confidence run away with them, particularly when things seem to be going well.

On a charge of conspiracy, one of the accused called several witnesses as to character. He kept his star witness to the end, a prosperous-looking man wearing a top hat and morning coat with a gardenia in his buttonhole. He had possibly decided to attire himself regardless of expense in the hope of impressing the jury.

The accused greeted him with a warm smile.

'I have been connected with you in various business transactions, have I not?' he asked confidently.

'You have.'

'Well,' (smiling slyly at the jury), 'in all these transactions have I not invariably conducted myself with the honesty and integrity of an English gentleman?'

The witness thought deeply.

'In no single instance,' he replied.

'No more questions,' said the accused faintly.

žžž   žžž   žžž

In a County Court action over the ownership of a donkey, both parties were costermongers and conducted their own cases with several fruity exchanges which are not fit to be reproduced in these delicate pages.

The case dragged on to such a length that the Judge at last said genially, 'Now, my men, I'm going to have my lunch and before I come back I hope you'll settle your dispute out of Court.'

When he returned, refreshed, the parties appeared before him, somewhat changed but in a friendlier spirit. The plaintiff now sported a ripe black eye, and the defendant had evidently had the claret tapped from his nose.

The defendant came forward, holding his nose but managing to smile.

'Well, your honour,' he said cheerfully, 'we've taken your advice. Jim's given me a damn good hiding and I've given him back his donkey.'

A story, now in some danger of becoming a classic and inevitably misquoted, concerns a certain very conscientious solicitor who won a hard-fought case. He thought it would be a nice gesture to wire the good news to his client who had been prevented by illness from attending and might be anxious as to the result.

'Justice has triumphed,' he cabled crisply.

He did not quite expect the reply, 'Appeal at once.'

Counsel was bullying a witness who kept side-stepping the steam roller.

'Do I understand you to say that the defendant made certain remarks about me?' demanded the barrister.

'Yes, I did say so.'

'Ah, I thought so! Can you substantiate these remarks?'

'No, sir, I don't think I can,' said the witness politely.

'Ah, something slanderous, I presume,' said Counsel contemptuously. 'Kindly tell the Court exactly what he said.'

'Well, sir,' the witness recalled amicably, 'he said you were an honest and truthful man.'

'That will do,' snapped Counsel. 'Call the next witness.'

▨   ▨   ▨

A magistrate at Brentford liked to rattle through his List. In an assault case he rapped out at the prosecutor: 'What evidence have you brought?'

'I have brought my black eye,' replied the man with simple dignity.

▨   ▨   ▨

During an action concerning a woman who had apparently been expelled from a convent without proper cause, the defendant declared emphatically that the plaintiff had offended her in many ways. For instance, by eating strawberries.

'Strawberries!' roared Counsel. 'What harm was there in that?'

'It was forbidden, sir,' said the defendant stoutly.

'Come, come,' smiled the learned man, 'what possible trouble was likely to come from eating strawberries?'

'Well, sir, you might ask what trouble was likely to

151

come from eating an apple, yet you should know what trouble *did* come from it.'

📖   📖   📖

A. E. Bowker, Clerk to Marshall Hall and Norman Birkett, has some wonderful stories to tell about his experiences. In *A Lifetime with the Law*, a mine of classic stories, he relates an anecdote which is always told against lawyers.

A certain solicitor, who belonged to a breed now becoming extinct, thanks among other factors to the vigilance of the Law Society, sent his client the following statement of costs:

'To crossing the Strand after seeing you on the
other side to discuss your case with you   .   .   6s.   8d.

To re-crossing the Strand after discovering the
person I saw was not you   .   .   .   .   6s.   8d.'

📖   📖   📖

That kindly old Judge, Mr. Justice Willes, was hearing an application in Chambers and found himself being badgered by a most persistent barrister. His lordship was weakening under the barrage but tried to put up some resistance.

'I'm one of the most obstinate men in the world,' he said, rather half-heartedly.

'God forbid that I should be so rude as to contradict your lordship,' rejoined Counsel.

📖   📖   📖

T. W. H. Crosland, the hard-drinking Bohemian poet and sworn enemy of Oscar Wilde, often landed in the Courts owing to his exuberant tongue and pen. He was a fascinating and agile witness who proved more than a match for cross-examiners.

Even the great F. E. Smith suffered at his hands.

'I am anxious that the jury should not be confused,' Crosland remarked.

'The jury can take care of themselves,' snapped F.E.

'I daresay they can,' agreed Crosland, 'but I want them to take care of *me*.'

Everybody in Court laughed, except Smith who tried to make himself heard.

Crosland pressed on. 'I am here to fight with one of the finest intellects in England. Two thousand quids' worth of Counsel against a poor man.' He turned on F.E. once again. 'You go on browbeating me. If you go on for another five hours, you will probably get me to say that I murdered Queen Anne.'

Counsel remarked that a man's works should be remembered and his life forgotten, referring pointedly to Wilde. Crosland punctured this with ridicule.

'As a man grows older, he will become riper,' he said genially. 'As you grow older, Mr. Smith, *you* will become riper.'

Crosland won the day and stepped jauntily from the dock.

◫   ◫   ◫

Wise the Counsel who smells a rat in time. Too many have

allowed themselves to be deceived by the Simple Simon in the box.

One witness, a rustic and apparently no Senior Wrangler, observed under cross-examination:

'My father had twice twenty children.'

Counsel from London raised his heavy eyebrows and twitched a smile at the jury. He turned back to his victim.

'Forty children!' he scoffed.

'No,' the witness corrected him gently. 'He had twenty children first of all. Then one died, making nineteen. Then he had another, making the twenty again. So there you have it! He had twice twenty!'

♕   ♕   ♕

At Norwich, a hardened poacher was charged with stealing a rabbit. The circumstantial evidence appeared to be overwhelming, but the jury did not think so, and brought in a verdict of 'Not Guilty'.

As the Judge acquitted him, the man stared across at the Bench with a look of utter amazement on his face.

'Well, I'm blowed,' he mumbled. Then he turned to his Counsel and called out, 'God bless you, sir.' To the jury, he shouted gaily, 'A merry Christmas to you all.'

♕   ♕   ♕

It has often proved costly to try and score off a woman witness, particularly a pretty one.

In a murder trial before Mr. Justice Grantham a key witness was giving evidence against the accused. She was a most decorative and elegantly dressed woman but obviously with little education. Counsel for the defence embarked on a series of searching questions which were deliberately offensive and designed to shake her under cross-examination.

The following remarkable dialogue followed:

Counsel: 'What are you?'

Witness: 'A woman.'

Counsel: 'I can see that. Are you married?'

Witness: 'No.'

Counsel: 'Are you single?'

Witness: 'No.'

Counsel: 'I beg your pardon. You are a widow?'

Witness: 'No.'

Counsel (angrily): 'Don't trifle with me!'

The Judge: 'She is not trifling.'

Counsel (raising his eyes to a merciful Heaven): 'Not married, not single, not a widow . . .' Then, with sudden inspiration, 'You must be engaged.'

Witness: 'No.'

Counsel (red in the face): 'Then what in Heaven's name are you?'

Witness (demurely): 'I am divorced.'

This was definitely not to be Counsel's red-letter day. Still smarting, he returned to the fray, sadder if not wiser.

'Does your husband allow you alimony?'

'No.'

'Then how do you live?'

'On food.' This reply set the jury chortling and the Judge blew his nose on a vast handkerchief.

'Yes, yes,' went on Counsel impatiently, 'but where do you get the money to buy the food?'

'I have an income,' said the lady serenely.

Counsel bristled with triumph and tried not to look at the jury. 'What is the source of it?' he demanded sharply.

The witness turned to the Judge and fluttered her lovely eyelashes. 'My lord, am I bound to answer these questions?' His lordship nodded. Counsel sharpened his scalpel and repeated the question.

'Well, I have a business,' said the lady.

At last the moment of truth. Counsel lunged forward.

'What—is—the—nature—of—your—business?' he asked, very slowly.

'I am a laundress.'

Counsel charged on to his Waterloo. With a pitying smile he demanded, 'Tell me the name of someone—any-one—whose linen you have washed in the last six months.'

'My own,' said the witness sweetly.

⚏　　⚏　　⚏

Counsel was finding the lady in the box extremely difficult to saw in half under cross-examination. Finally, he resorted to the old offensive question:

'Do you know what the truth is, madam?'

'Am I bound to answer that?' she appealed to Judge Tudor Rees. He nodded.

'Well,' she said thoughtfully, 'truth is the virtue made

manifest in the answers I have given to your irrelevant questions. But, of course, it would be too much to expect you to recognize it.'

* * *

The Divorce Courts provide much that is sordid and depressing. Sometimes, however, the lighter side of life appears, usually without intention.

In one case, the co-respondent had firmly denied the allegations and appeared to be the innocent victim of a grave slur on his good name. Unfortunately for him, he turned out to be a trifle naïve.

'You were friendly with the respondent for many years?' he was asked.

'Yes,' he nodded politely.

'You often went to dinners and dances together?' Another nod of agreement.

'You spent week-ends at Brighton together?' He nodded unsuspectingly.

'Have you ever slept with the lady?'

'No, sir,' he replied emphatically and without hesitation. 'Not a wink!'

* * *

At the Assizes in the West Country, a beefy man with the shoulders of a bull denied indignantly that he had committed assault and battery upon one of his neighbours. He was most emphatic that he had nothing but the milk of human kindness flowing through his veins.

He addressed the Bench with outraged innocence.

'My lord, how can I be called a quarrelsome man when I've been bound over twenty-three times to keep the peace?'

　　　　　📖　　📖　　📖

In another case of assault one of the witnesses appeared to be rather less than frank. Counsel eyed him disdainfully.

'So you saw these two men fighting?' he drawled. 'And yet you did not see fit to go to the assistance of the prosecutor.'

The witness snorted. 'And how was I to know which was going to be the prosecutor?' he objected.

　　　　　📖　　📖　　📖

Jack Johnson, the negro fighter, proved himself quite a warrior at Bow Street. He appeared with Billy Wells, whom he was due to fight at Earl's Court under the auspices of Jimmy White, the financier. Under a militant clergyman, public feeling was whipped up to prevent the fight taking place. This clergyman threatened to travel up to Balmoral where Winston Churchill, the Home Secretary, was the guest of King Edward. With the Bishop of London, he intended to present a petition against holding the fight.

Mr. Churchill stopped the visit with a characteristic

telegram: 'Matter is receiving close attention. Shall be very glad to receive memorial by post but do not consider it necessary to ask you and the Bishop of London to undertake such a pilgrimage.'

Nothing daunted, the diehards managed to get the boxers and the promoter charged with threatening to commit a breach of the peace. No less a personage than Sir John Simon, the Solicitor-General, led for the Crown.

Johnson defended himself and did very well, as always.

'Have you ever seen a boxing contest?' he asked a police witness.

'No.'

'You have no idea what they are?'

'No.'

Johnson flashed a grin at the magistrate. 'The witness may go. I'm through.'

In the course of his address, the Solicitor-General remarked: 'I do not know exactly what a kidney punch is.'

'I'll show you,' volunteered Jack Johnson.

Counsel hurriedly declined the invitation.

꧁ ꧁ ꧁

The accused had the face of an elderly choirboy and a manner that was entirely episcopal. The Judge found it hard to believe that this man was a hardened thief.

'Not only did you take all the money from the drawer, but it seems that you also helped yourself to a quantity of valuable jewellery,' he said severely.

'That is so, my lord,' said the seraphic one, 'but you will

appreciate I was always taught that money alone does not bring happiness.'

⚏   ⚏   ⚏

Before it was pulled down and rebuilt, the Old Bailey's acoustics were far from perfect; indeed, the echo in some Courts was far worse than anything at the Royal Albert Hall.

At the end of one trial, the Judge sentenced the prisoner to seven years' penal servitude. The wretched man called his Counsel over and seemed very agitated.

'Did his lordship give me fourteen years?' he stammered.

'No, certainly not. Only seven.'

'Well,' said the man, relieved but still very puzzled, 'I could have sworn that I heard him say seven years, *twice*.'

⚏   ⚏   ⚏

This could only have happened in an Irish Court. Daniel O'Connor was eloquently defending a man on a charge of murder when the 'corpse', very much alive and obviously in social mood, lurched into Court.

When the excitement had died down, the Judge asked the jury to return their inevitable verdict. To his and everyone else's amazement, they found the accused 'Guilty'.

'But,' thundered the Judge, tugging at his collar which had suddenly become very tight, 'the alleged murdered man is here alive.'

'That may be so,' said the foreman stoutly, 'but all I know is that the prisoner stole my brown mare.'

* * *

Sir Chartres Biron, the genial Bow Street magistrate, always had a major share of drunks before him. One old woman charged with being drunk had been found sitting on the pavement.

She pleaded most vehemently that it was not the strength of the refreshment but the weakness in her legs that had caused her to collapse. She fixed the magistrate with an inviting eye, slightly bloodshot.

'As to the pure all things are pure,' she said solemnly, 'I should like you to see me in your private room and satisfy yourself by personal inspection that my statements are true.'

Sir Chartres declined and found the charge proved.

* * *

Another lady with a remarkable thirst produced a highly novel defence.

'No, I don't deny being drunk, your worship,' she said warmly, 'but I know you will be lenient with me because I was the very first woman to stand in this 'ere dock when this Court was built. I christened it, so to speak. Aren't I right, gaoler? Speak up like a man!'

She was always let off lightly but, after a few years, this odd 'godmother' had to pay her fines just like the others.

At the Cambridge Assizes appeared a farmer who had killed his wife after a violent quarrel. Apparently, he had come home from market, very drunk, and demanded his tea. His wife refused to give him any and ordered him to go to bed and sleep it off. He struck her a heavy blow which proved fatal.

After the inevitable verdict of manslaughter, one of the jurymen turned to his neighbour and said feelingly:

'Terrible thing to kill your wife for a cup of tea.'

'Yes,' said his colleague solemnly, 'but there is nothing so aggravating as a woman who refuses to make a cup when you're dry.'

෴ ෴ ෴

A young barrister, defending a man charged with stealing a pair of trousers, pleaded his cause so shrewdly and eloquently that he secured an acquittal in the teeth of the evidence. The Court rose but not the defendant who seemed in no hurry to leave the dock.

'You are free, my man,' said Counsel, picking up his papers. 'You can leave now.'

'I'd rather wait until the prosecutor leaves the Court.'

'Why?'

'Because I have them on,' explained his client.

෴ ෴ ෴

A magistrate became very irritable with a voluble witness

who kept straying from the questions to address the Court himself.

'Are you going to act as your wife's Counsel in this case?' demanded his worship.

'I am no Counsel,' said the witness. 'I only speak the truth.'

᠎ ♖ ♖ ♖

An old Etonian had delighted the Court with his courtesy and wit but this, unhappily, did not prevent the Judge from giving him a severe sentence for obtaining money by false pretences. His father, a most respectable pillar of society, was heartbroken. The young man put a consoling arm round him before he went below and said, 'I'll write as soon as I get a moment, my dear pater.'

He kept his word in a letter from Parkhurst, addressed to his unhappy mamma.

'Give my love to poor father. I feel sure he will be pleased to know that whereas I am the only Old Etonian here, there are at least three Old Harrovians.'

♖ ♖ ♖

A certain barrister was one of the terrors of the Old Bailey and notorious, in particular, for his gift for trapping unwary witnesses.

'You say that the prisoner is a thief?' he asked sharply.

'Yes,' said the witness. 'She confessed it.'

'And you swear that she went on working for you after she confessed it?'

'I do, sir.'

Counsel glanced triumphantly at the jury before glaring at his victim.

'We are given to understand that you employ dishonest people to work for you, even after their characters and reputations are known?' he demanded with scorn.

'Of course,' agreed the witness. 'How else could I get assistance from a lawyer?'

❦ ❦ ❦

The accused had been found guilty and there was the usual hush while the Judge gazed sternly upon him.

'Prisoner, have you anything to say in your defence before I pass sentence?' he demanded very deliberately.

The prisoner fixed the Bench with a winning smile. 'Your lordship sees that I have engaged no lawyer to defend me, and I trust this mitigating circumstance will be taken into account.'

❦ ❦ ❦

A man was charged with being drunk and disorderly in Trafalgar Square. Drunk, yes, but disorderly, definitely not, he insisted with dignity.

The magistrate asked the policeman exactly how the accused had been disorderly.

'Well, your worship, he was kissing the lions,' was the simple reply.

❦ ❦ ❦

Gervais Rentoul, the West London magistrate, asked a prosecutor, 'Is it true, as alleged, that you declared that the prisoner had stolen your pocket-book?'

The man shook his head solemnly.

'Your honour, I did not go as far as that. I merely said that if the prisoner had not assisted me in looking for the pocket-book, I might have found it.'

　　　🂠　　　🂠　　　🂠

One of the most impudent letters ever read out in a Court of Law was written by the 'Brides in the Bath' murderer, George Joseph Smith. His father-in-law had inquired about his background and Smith wrote back in the following terms:

'Sir—In answer to your application regarding my parentage, my mother was a bus-horse, my father a cab-driver, my sister a rough rider over the Arctic Regions. My brothers were all gallant sailors on a steam-roller.'

　　　🂠　　　🂠　　　🂠

Richard Muir, iron-hard Treasury Counsel, was a deadly prosecutor and the terror of the underworld. One day at the Old Bailey he collapsed from the heat. A barrister walked in and asked anxiously, 'What's the matter with Muir? Has he really fainted?'

'Yes,' said his learned friend. 'The prisoner has just been acquitted.'

At the Old Bailey a man accused of embezzlement asked for a 'dock brief'. He was invited to take his choice from the advocates in Court.

He at once chose a K.C. who could not, of course, appear without a junior. The prisoner then chose an alert-looking gentleman who turned out to be prosecuting Counsel. Finally, with an air of triumph, he pointed to a neat figure at the back.

'I'll have that gentleman,' he proclaimed. But that gentleman turned out to be a woman barrister which did not please the accused one bit.

He addressed the Bench. 'Blimey, it's worse than trying to pick a winner,' he said with feeling.

᙮ ᙮ ᙮

On circuit, a Judge was hearing a divorce action and finding that the petitioner had some difficulty in expressing herself clearly.

'What exactly *are* your grounds for this petition?' he asked kindly.

'Refined cruelty, my lord.'

'And what does that mean?' asked the Judge, perplexed.

'My husband tried to strangle me.'

᙮ ᙮ ᙮

Old George was a well-known character at Bow Street on charges of begging, loitering and kindred offences. The police did not like bringing him in because he was a like-

able scamp; besides which, he was the scourge of magistrates whose time he delighted in wasting.

Among his numerous talents was a gift for cross-talk repartee which would have been more usefully employed on the music-halls.

The following dialogue was typical of his performances in Court.

Magistrate: 'How do you live?'

George: 'Pretty well, sir. Generally, a joint and two veg for dinner.'

'I mean, how do you get your bread?'

'I beg your worship's pardon. Sometimes at the baker's and sometimes at the dairy, if I'm late.'

The magistrate (beginning to purple): 'You may think you are being funny but I don't. I simply mean to ask how you do?'

'Fairly well,' said George. 'I hope your worship is well.'

♛   ♛   ♛

Another old reprobate at Bow Street had sunk owing to his intense dislike of water either as a beverage or for ablutions. That sentimental magistrate, old Sir Henry Curtis Bennett, father of the famous K.C., choosing his words very carefully, addressed him with a sigh of regret.

'I am sorry to see you here again, for I take a great interest in you. You come of a good family and, as I know, your father was a most respected man in the City. In the circumstances, I shall send you to prison for only a month.'

'Only a month!' echoed the prisoner, slightly stunned. 'Thank goodness, you didn't know my grandfather.'

॥   ॥   ॥

At Petty Sessions, Counsel remarked to a policeman that the magistrates were getting through the List with remarkable speed and efficiency.

'Yes,' agreed the officer. 'Their worships always dispense with justice very fast here.'

॥   ॥   ॥

A well-known bankrupt whose name had recently appeared in all the newspapers hailed a taxi from his mansion and asked to be driven to Carey Street. He paid the fare and counted out a grudging sixpence in coppers as a tip.

'Well, I hope you get your discharge,' said the driver. 'At least, they can't say that extravagance has done it.'

॥   ॥   ॥

At Marylebone, the genial Mr. Plowden used a shrewd and kindly wit but not always at the expense of the sinners whose weaknesses had brought them to judgment. He was once asked how he managed to deal so swiftly and surely with the business of the Court. With a straight face he replied: 'It's all very simple and an ideal arrangement. My Clerk listens without deciding, while I decide without listening.'

In one case he had before him a woman charged with

being drunk and disorderly. With some indignation she swore that she was not only innocent of the particular charge but was, in fact, a lifelong teetotaller.

For the prosecution appeared a dour constable who was quite emphatic that she was absolutely unable to stand when he took her into custody.

'But what made you think she was drunk?' asked the magistrate keenly.

'She couldn't stand, sir,' replied the constable.

Mr. Plowden shook his wise old head. 'A lot of people can't stand but they are not drunk,' he observed.

Turning with a smile to the accused, he said gently, 'If you are a teetotaller and fall about the streets, you must take the risks.'

✺ ✺ ✺

But even Mr. Plowden was shaken on one occasion after he had fined a man twenty shillings for being drunk and incapable. A few minutes later, the man came rushing back into Court, looking very flushed and anxious.

'Excuse me, sir,' he burst out, 'but would you mind giving me a receipt for the pound I've just paid. My wife will never believe I didn't spend all my money on drink.'

✺ ✺ ✺

This same magistrate found himself at a social gathering and his host, a barrister, asked him if he had ever tried gin and ginger beer.

'No,' said Mr. Plowden, 'but I've tried a lot of chaps who have.'

⚏ ⚏ ⚏

At Marlborough Street appeared the perfect sea lawyer. The magistrate sized him up and decided to waste no time.

'Do you think you were sober?' he demanded briskly.

The accused smiled with infinite wisdom. 'When I'm drunk and know I'm drunk, then I'm sober. But when I'm drunk and think I'm sober, then I'm drunk.'

⚏ ⚏ ⚏

Finally, a story which all laymen—particularly unsuccessful litigants—will relish. The great Lord Chief Justice Coleridge was in a hurry and called a cab.

'Take me as quickly as possible to the Courts of Justice.'

'Where are they?' asked the man.

'What! You, a London cabby and don't know where the Law Courts are!'

'Oh! The Law Courts! I thought you said the Courts of Justice.'

⚏ ⚏ ⚏